How to View a 3D Stereogram

Take a pencil, bring it to your eyes. The idea is to make your eyes look behind the pencil and, instead of a pencil, you will see 2 pencils. Is this what we want. Move the focus of the eyes behind the real image. When looking at objects very closely, it is easy to get your eyes out of focus. But, a stereogram can best be seen at about 40 cm from the eyes, so it is much more difficult to focus away from the actual stereogram.

If you are not able to observe stereograms, this may take some time.

The first time I looked at a stereogram, it took me about an hour to finally focus my eyes correctly to see the 3D image.

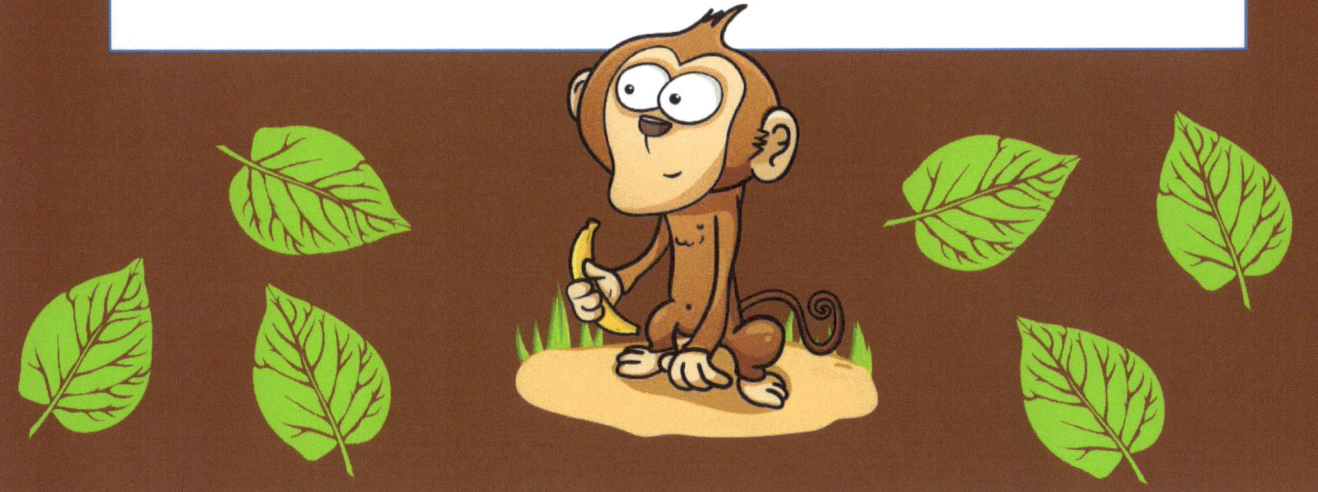

Bring the stereogram image very close to your eyes (until you touch it with your nose). At this distance, your eyes cannot focus on the image and look somewhere behind the image. Now slowly push the image away from you, while trying to keep your eyes out of focus. At some point you will see the hidden image.

Another method is to take an object and put it behind the image (about half a meter behind it). Now focus on the object behind the image while keeping your eyes looking at the image.

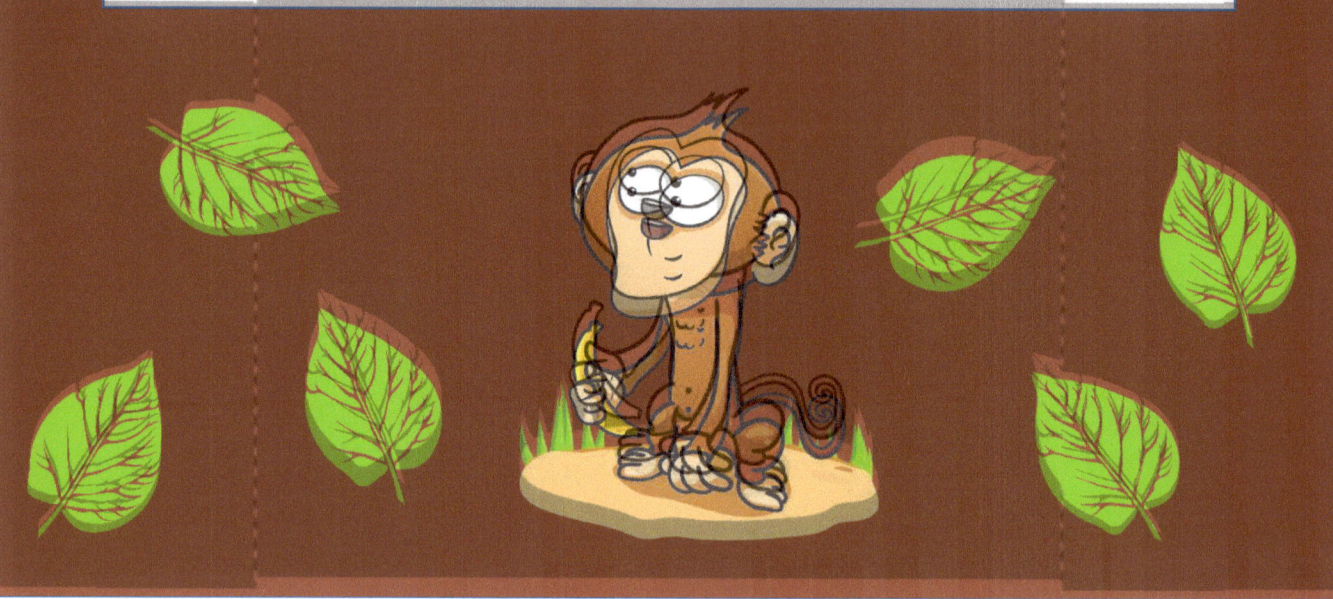

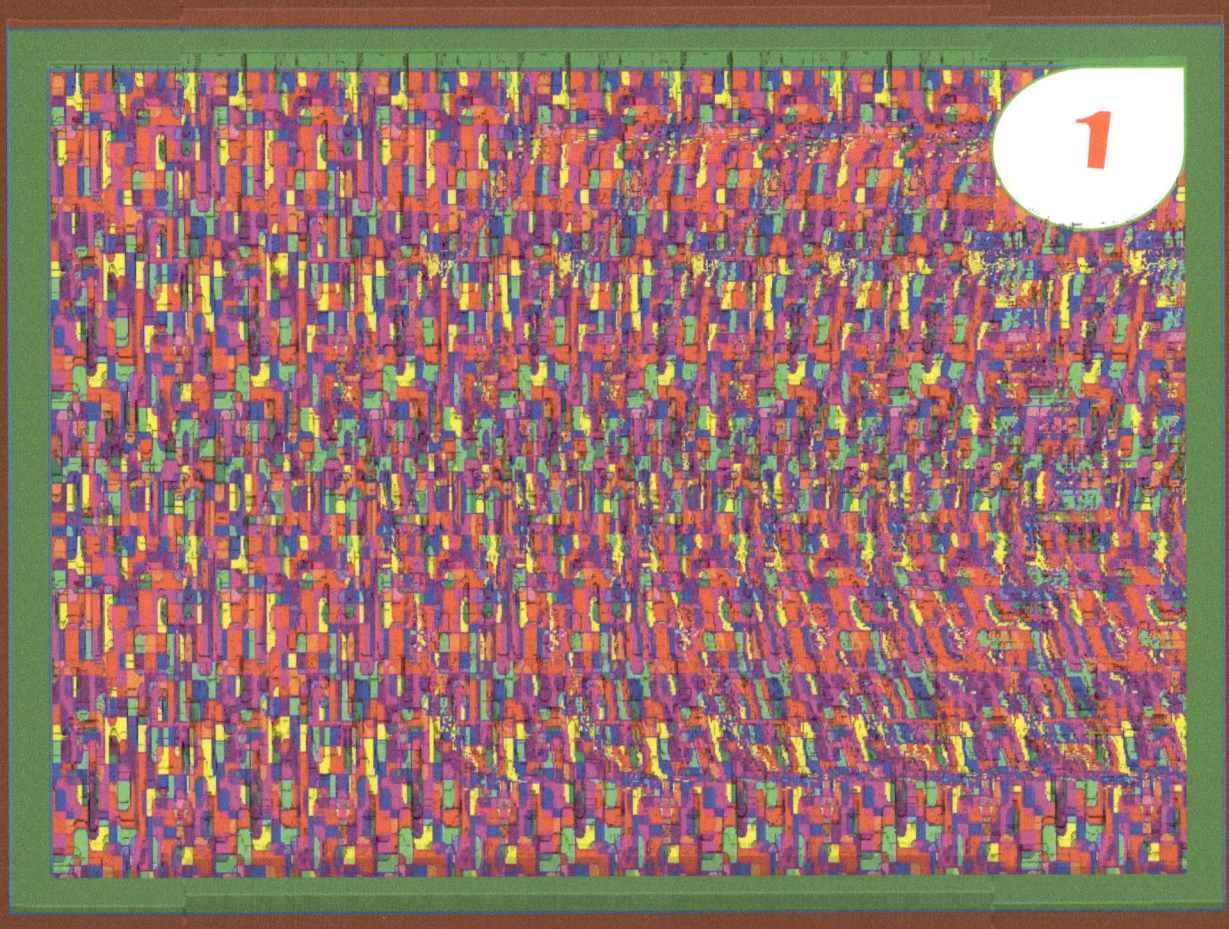

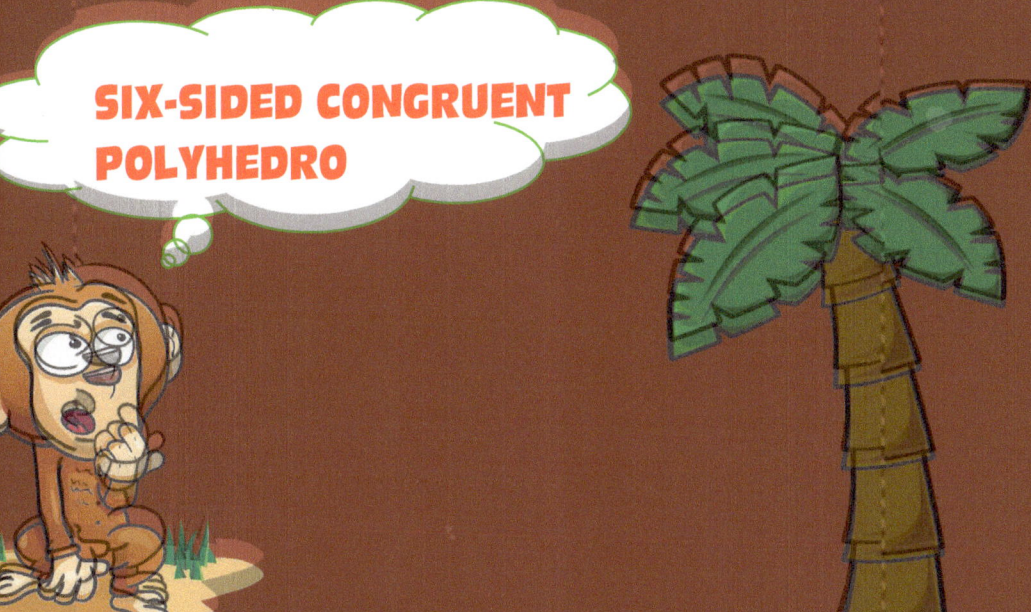

SIX-SIDED CONGRUENT POLYHEDRO

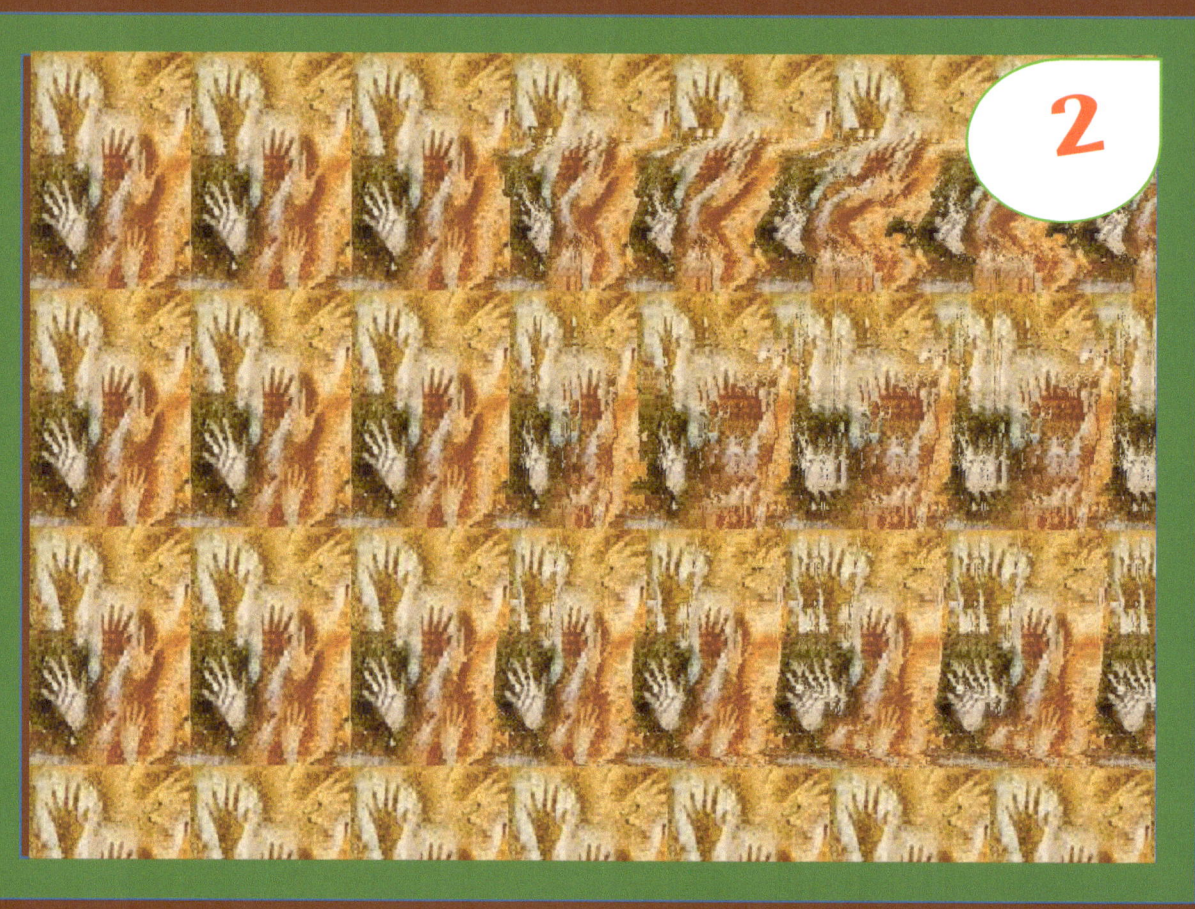

2

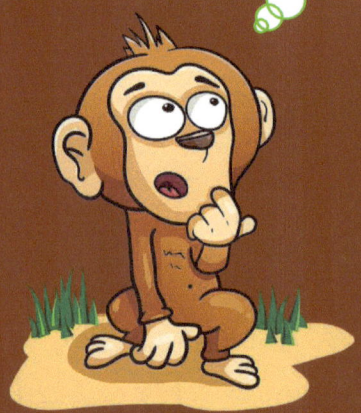

MEASURES TIME WITH SAND

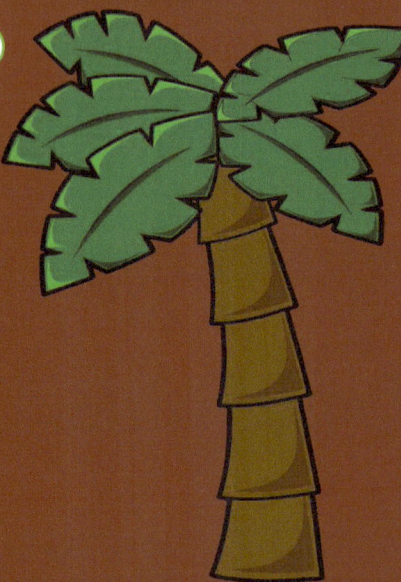

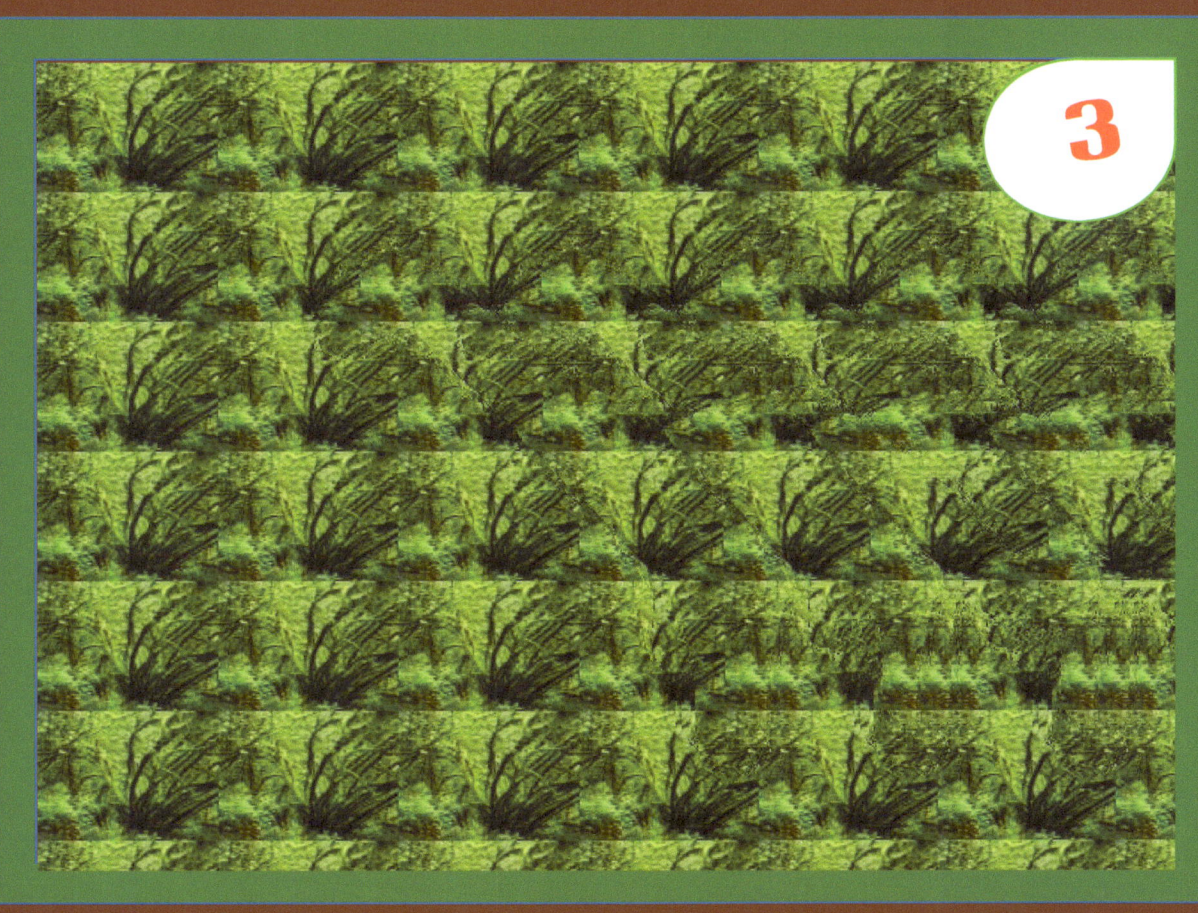

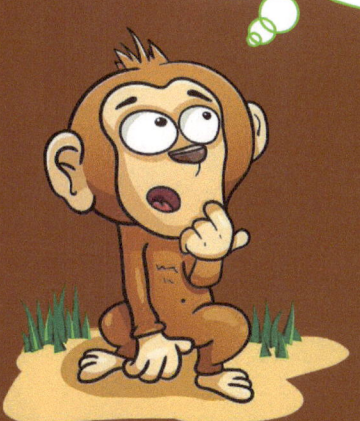

THEY LIVED MILLIONS OF YEARS AGO

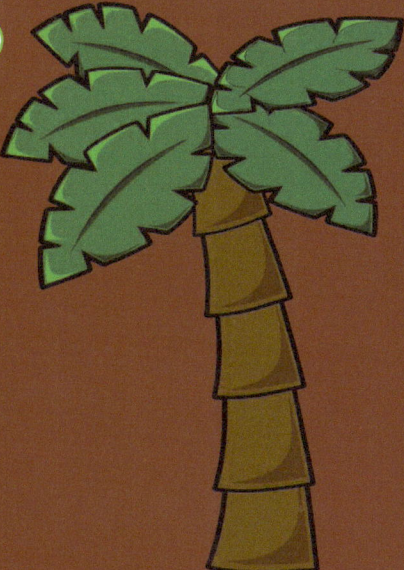

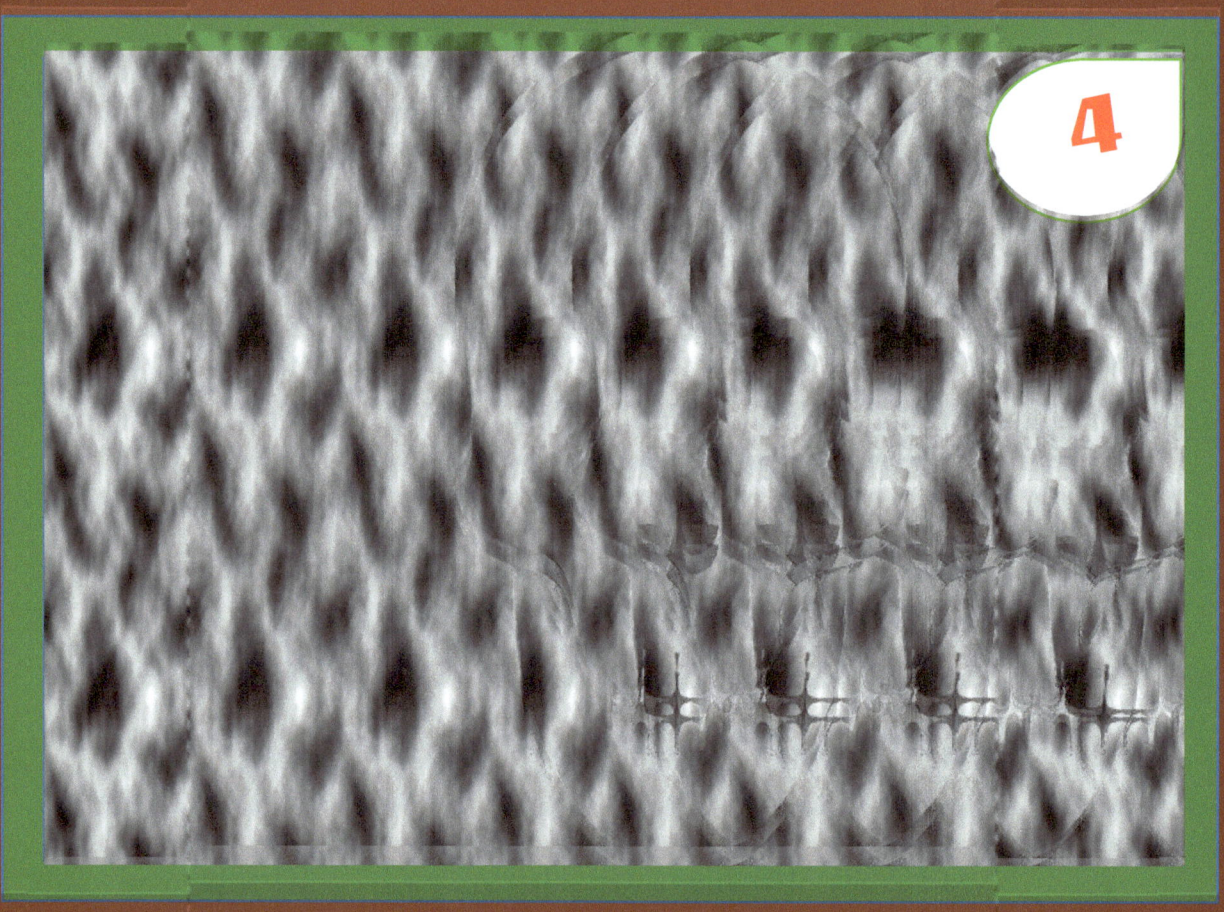

4

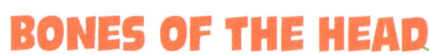

BONES OF THE HEAD

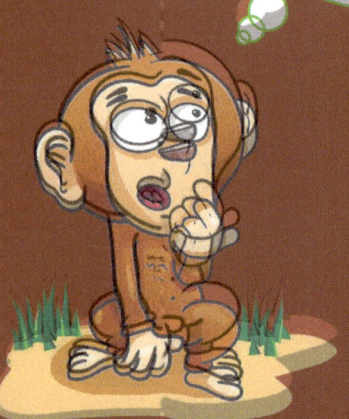
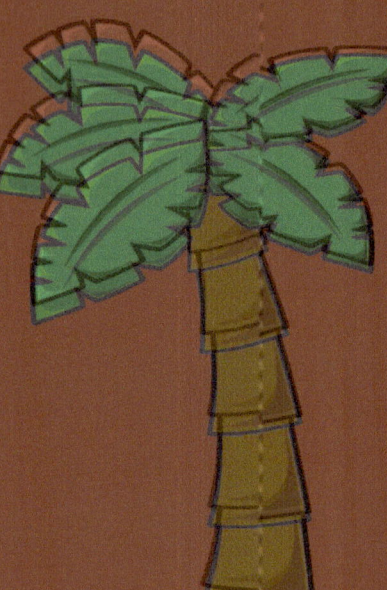

5

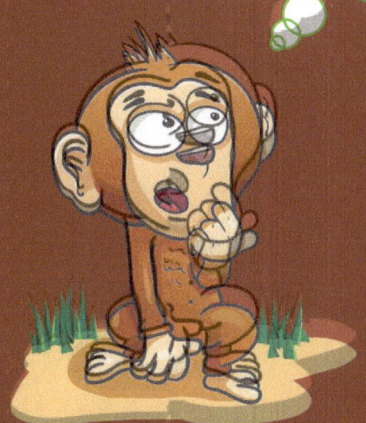

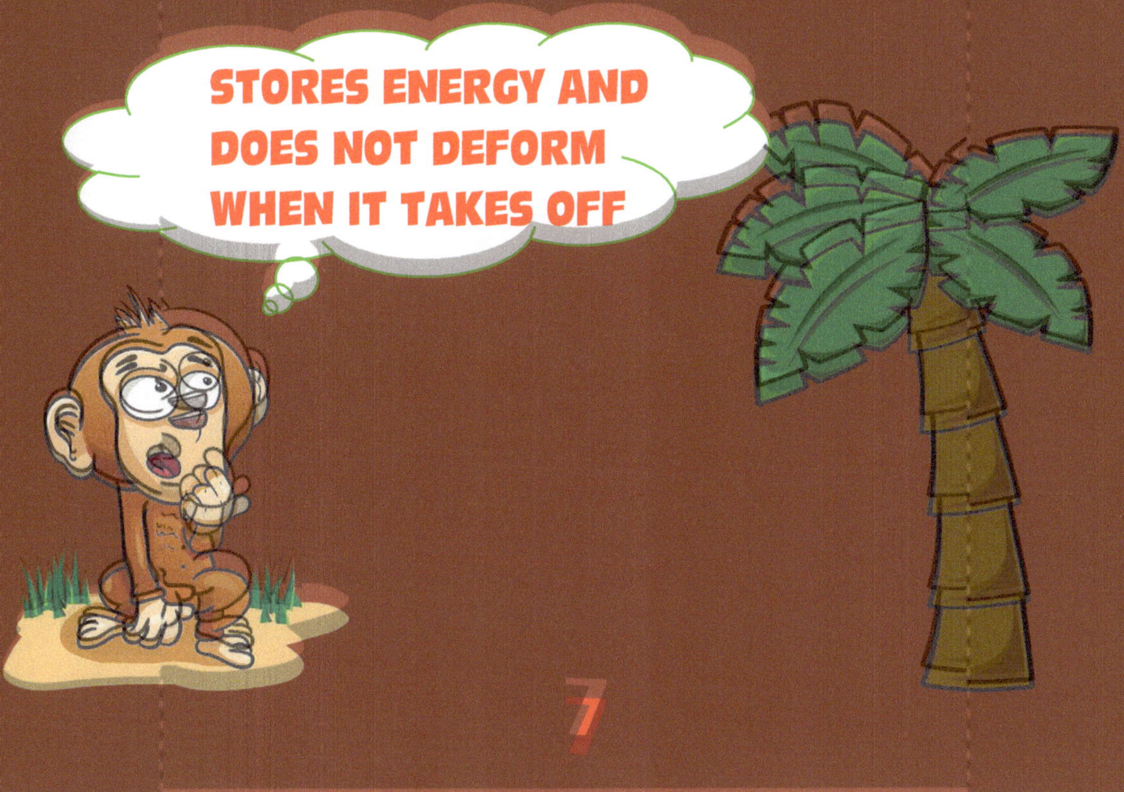

STORES ENERGY AND DOES NOT DEFORM WHEN IT TAKES OFF

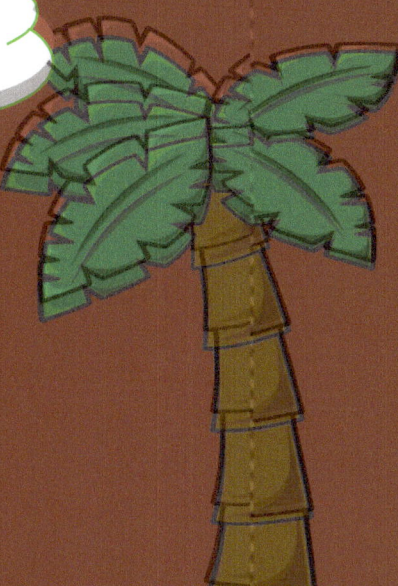

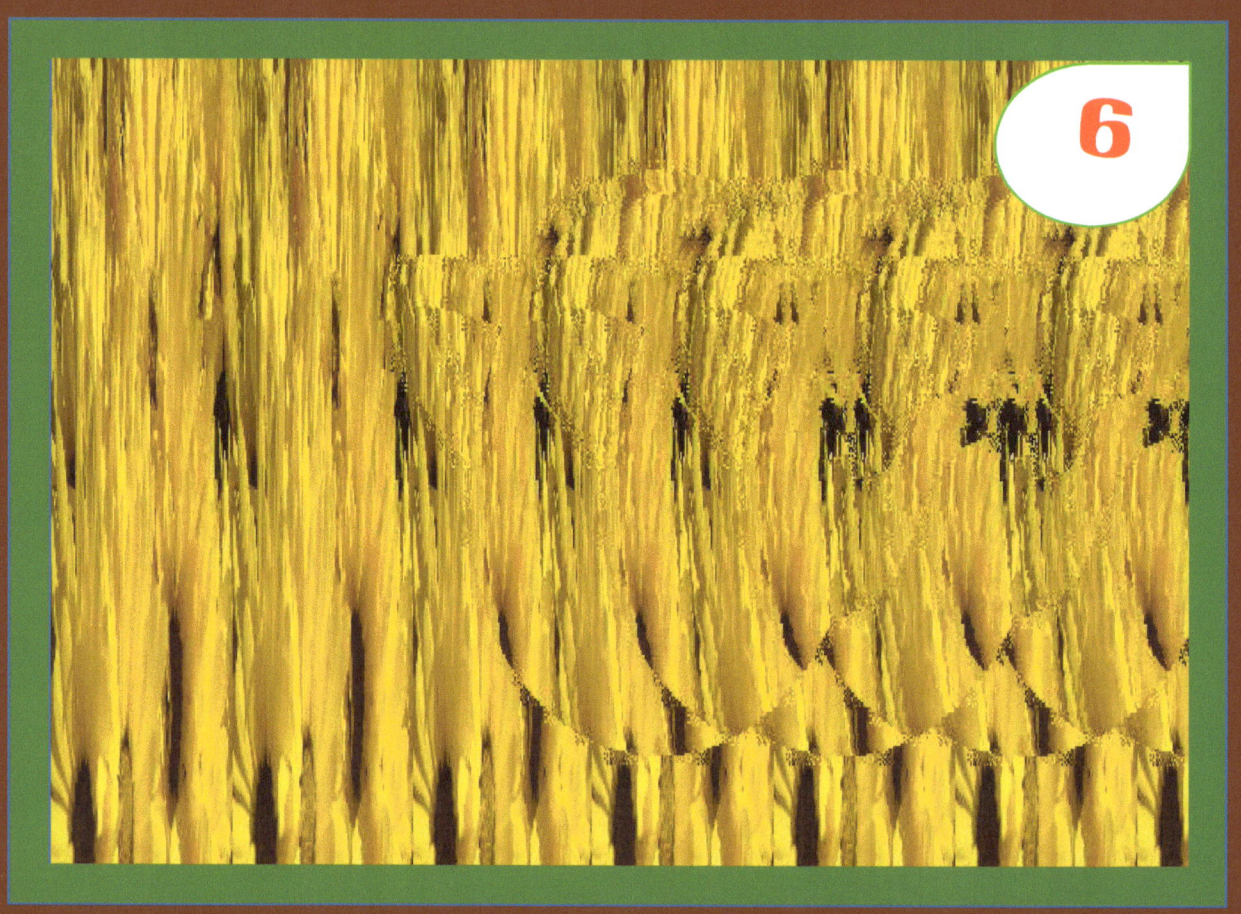

6

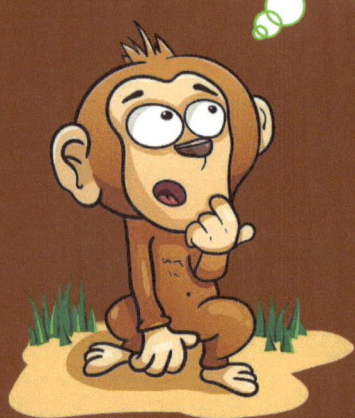

CONTAINER WHERE THE WATER IS BOILED

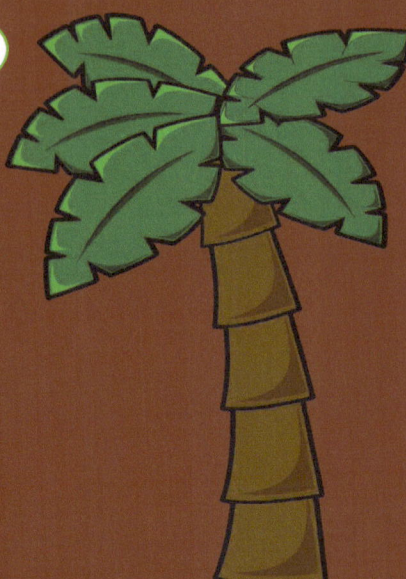

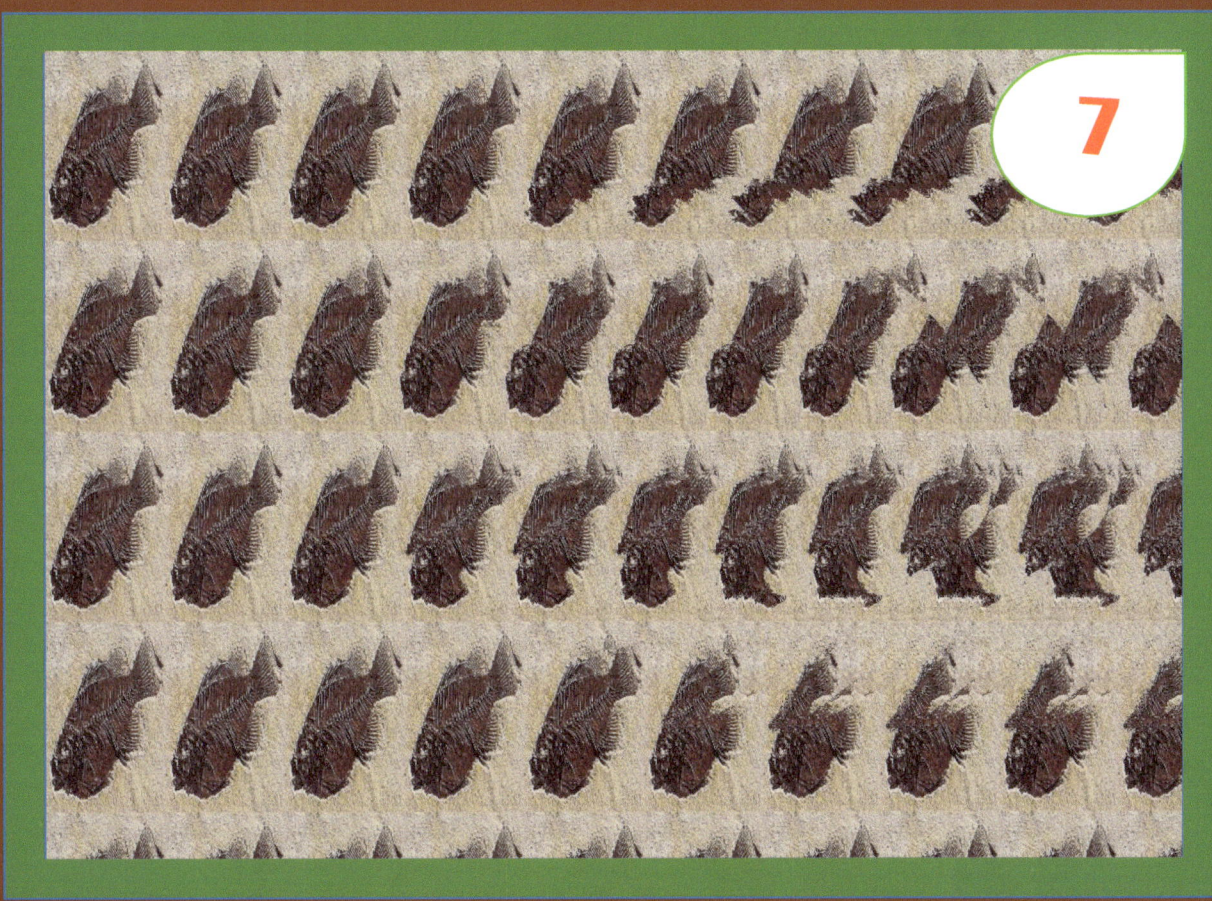

7

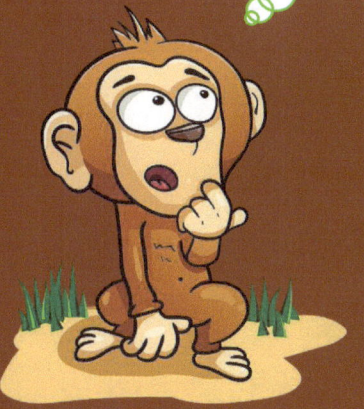

LIVES IN THE SEA

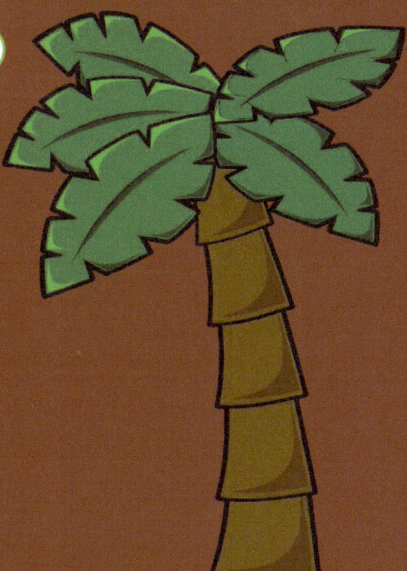

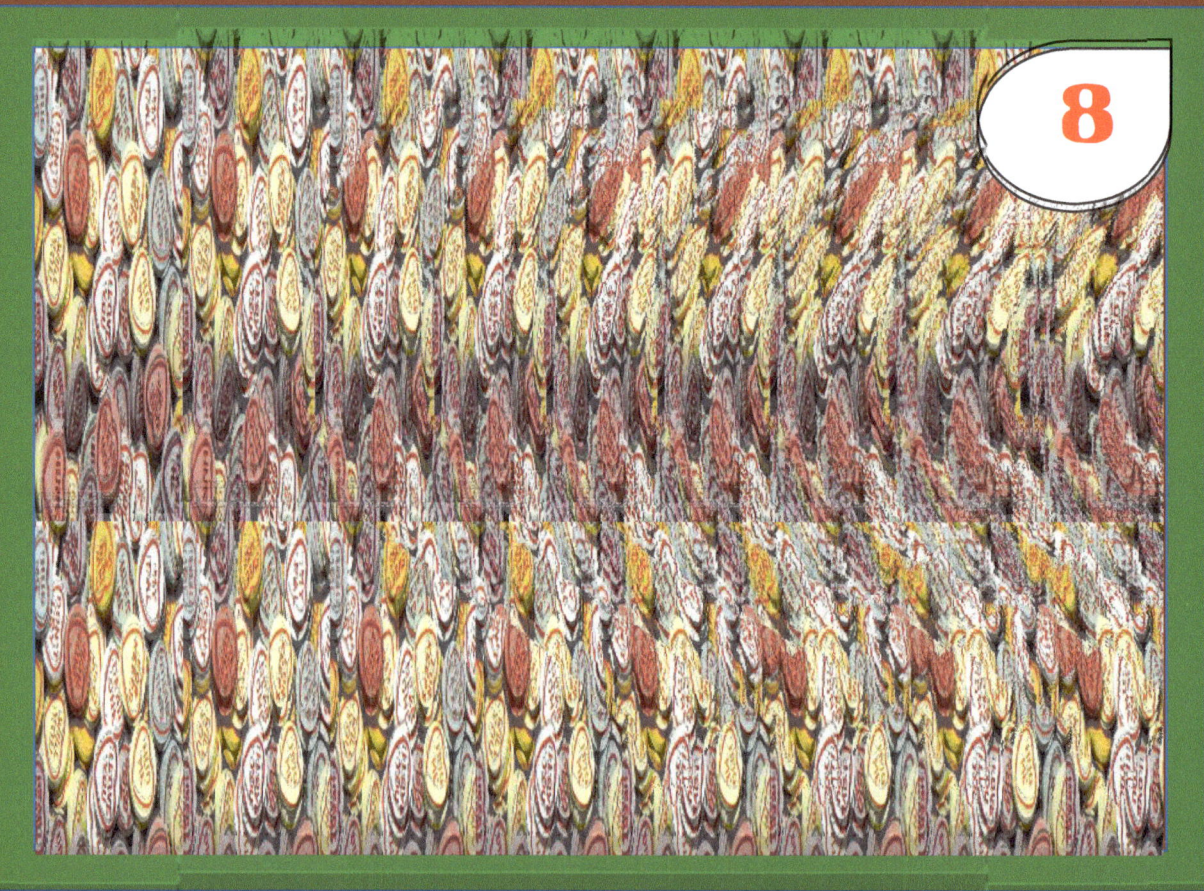

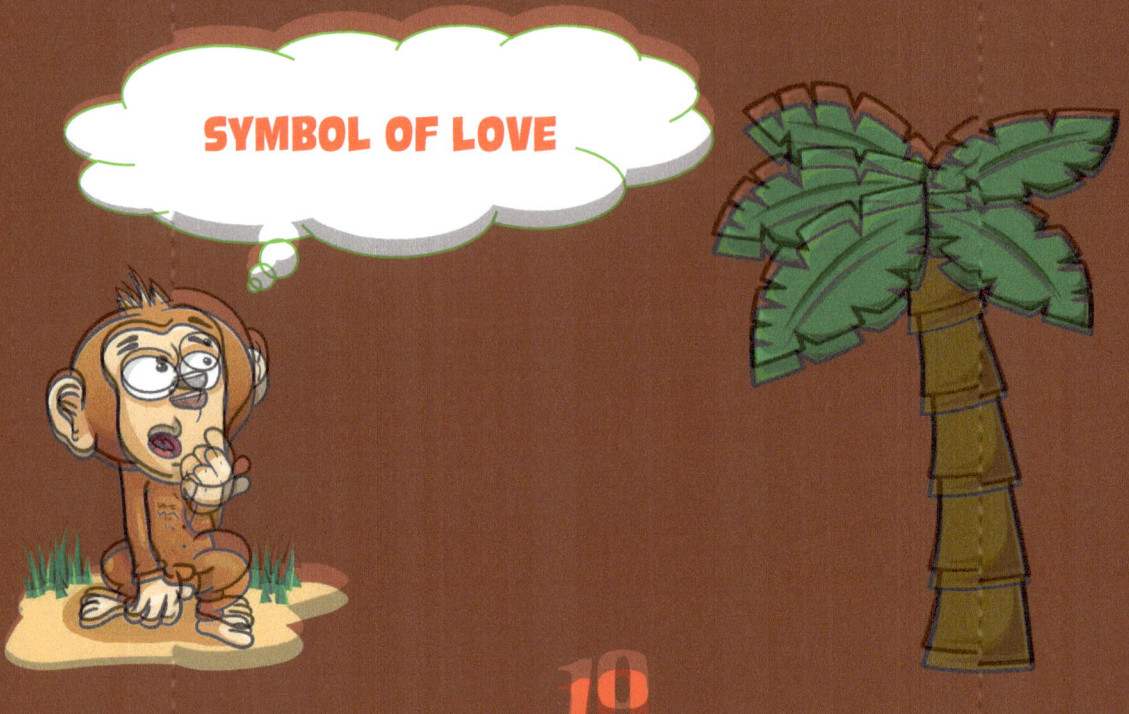

SYMBOL OF LOVE

9

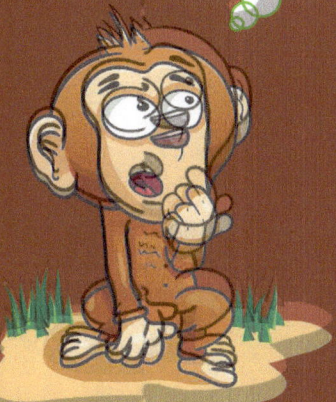

FLYING MACHINE

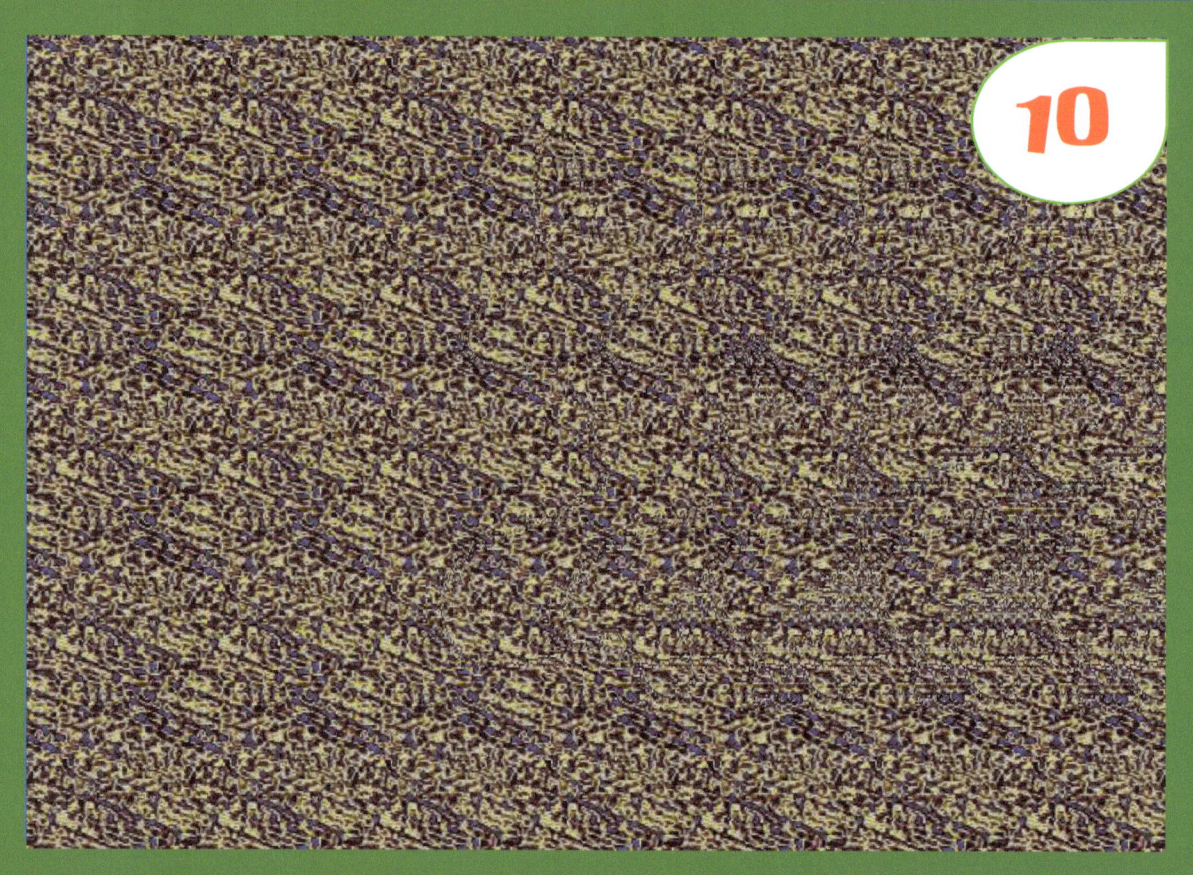

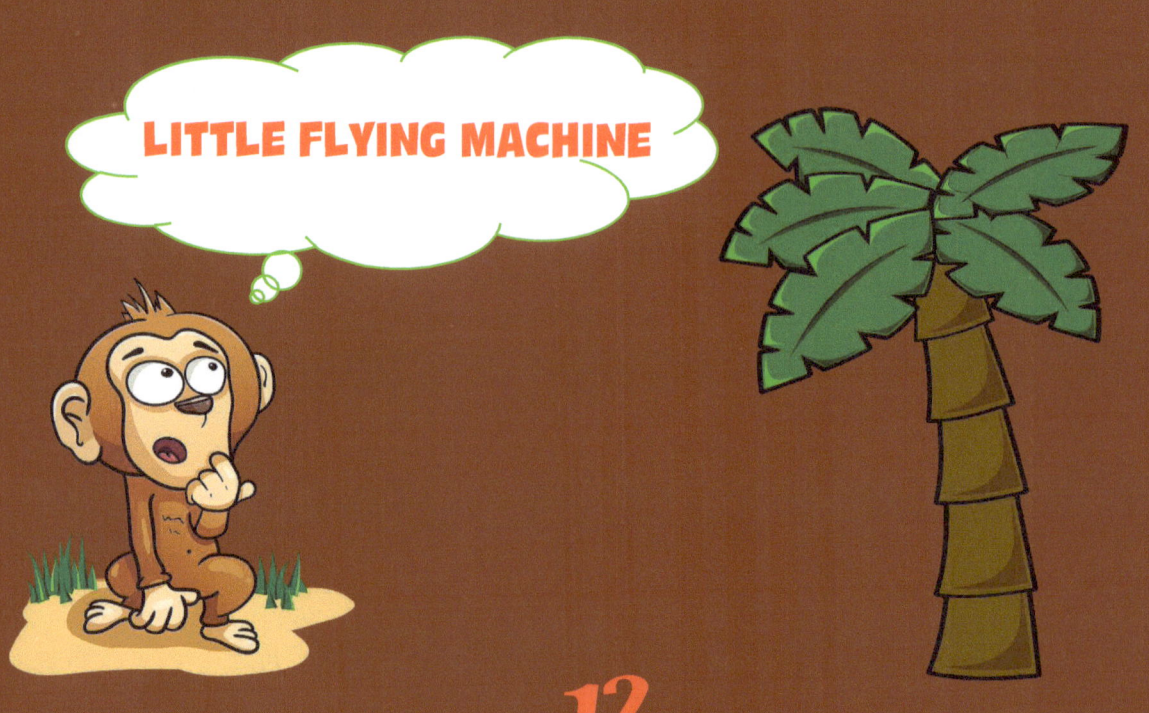

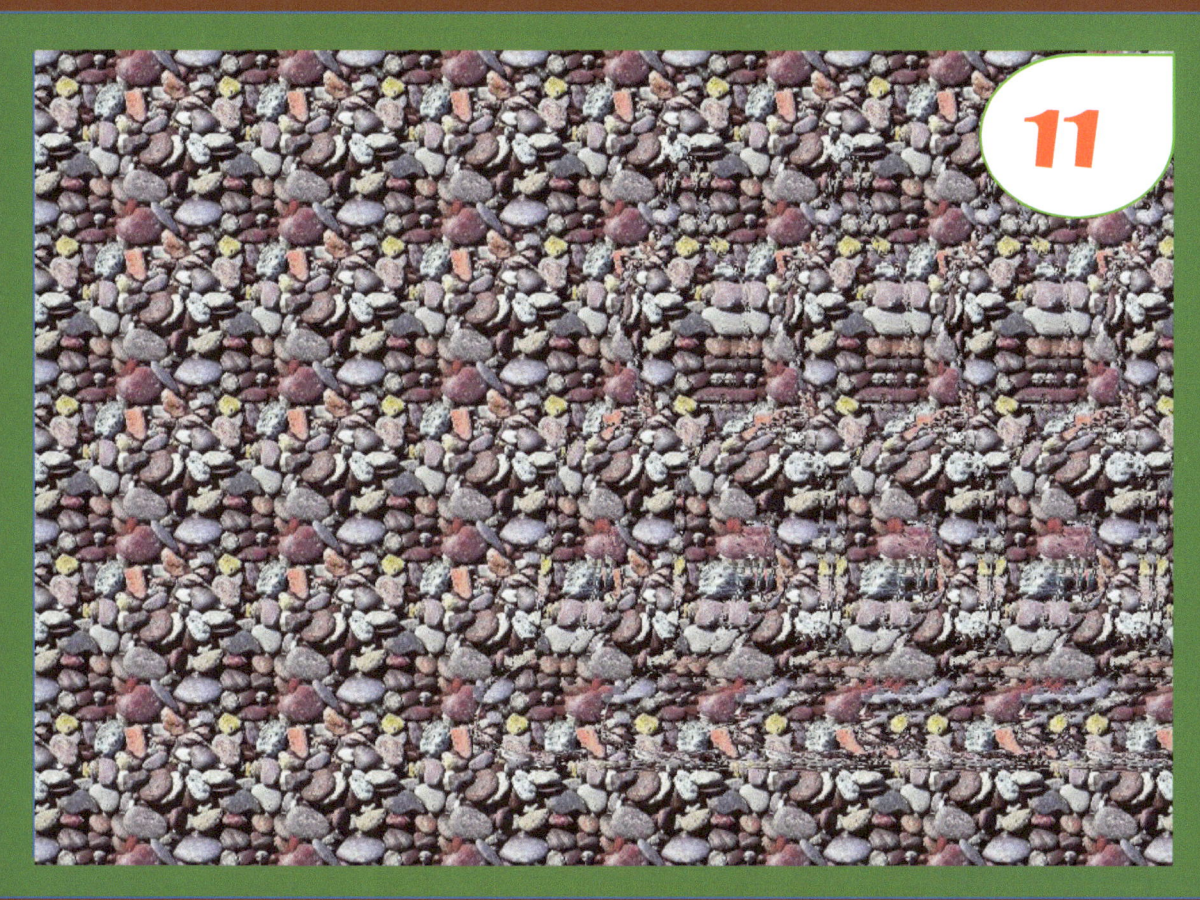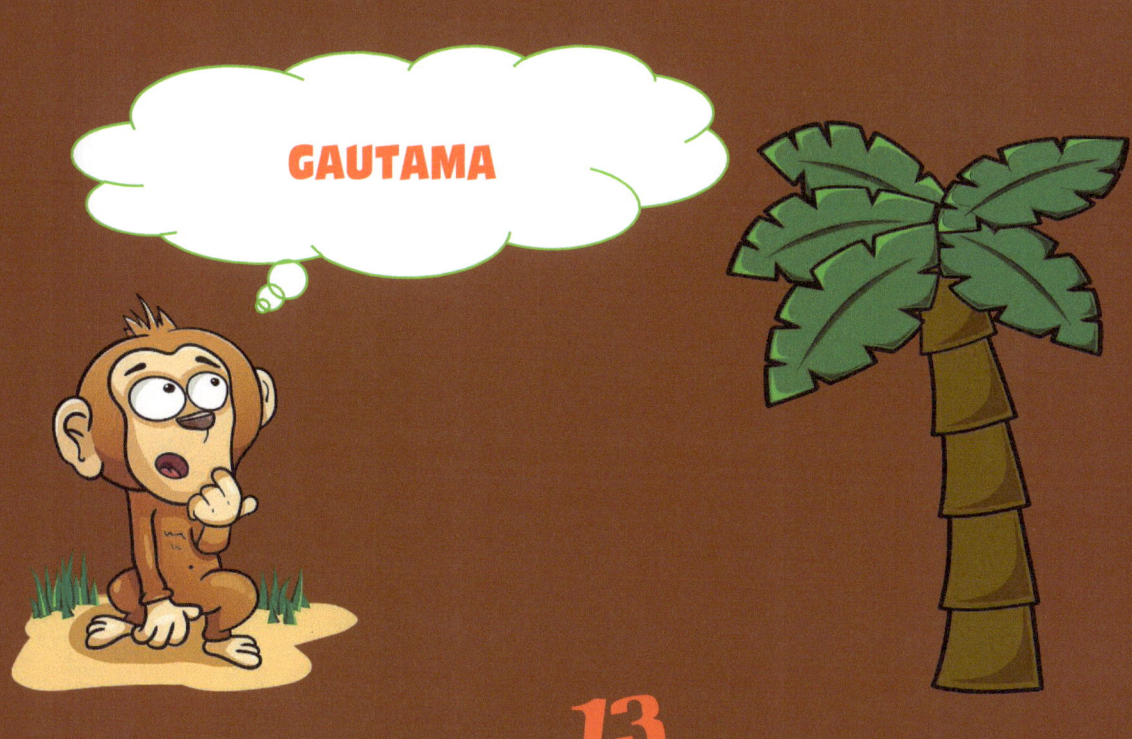

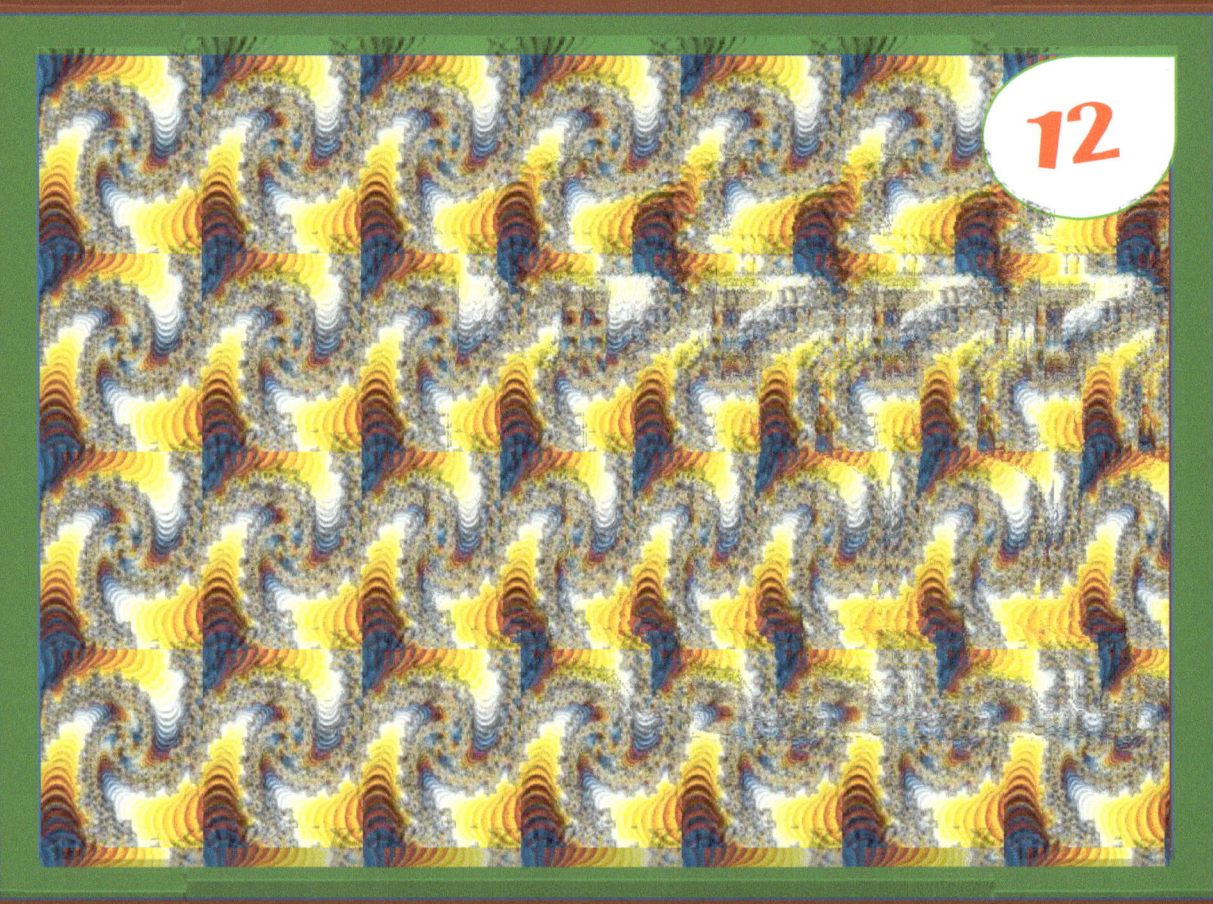

12

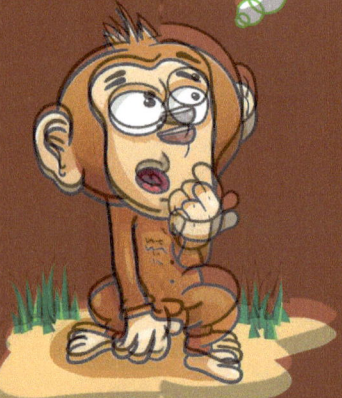

RUN ON THE RAIL

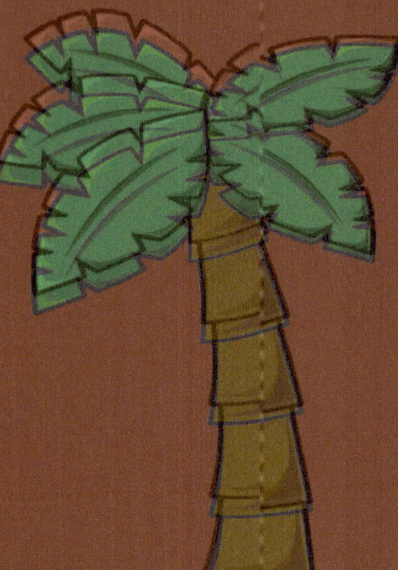

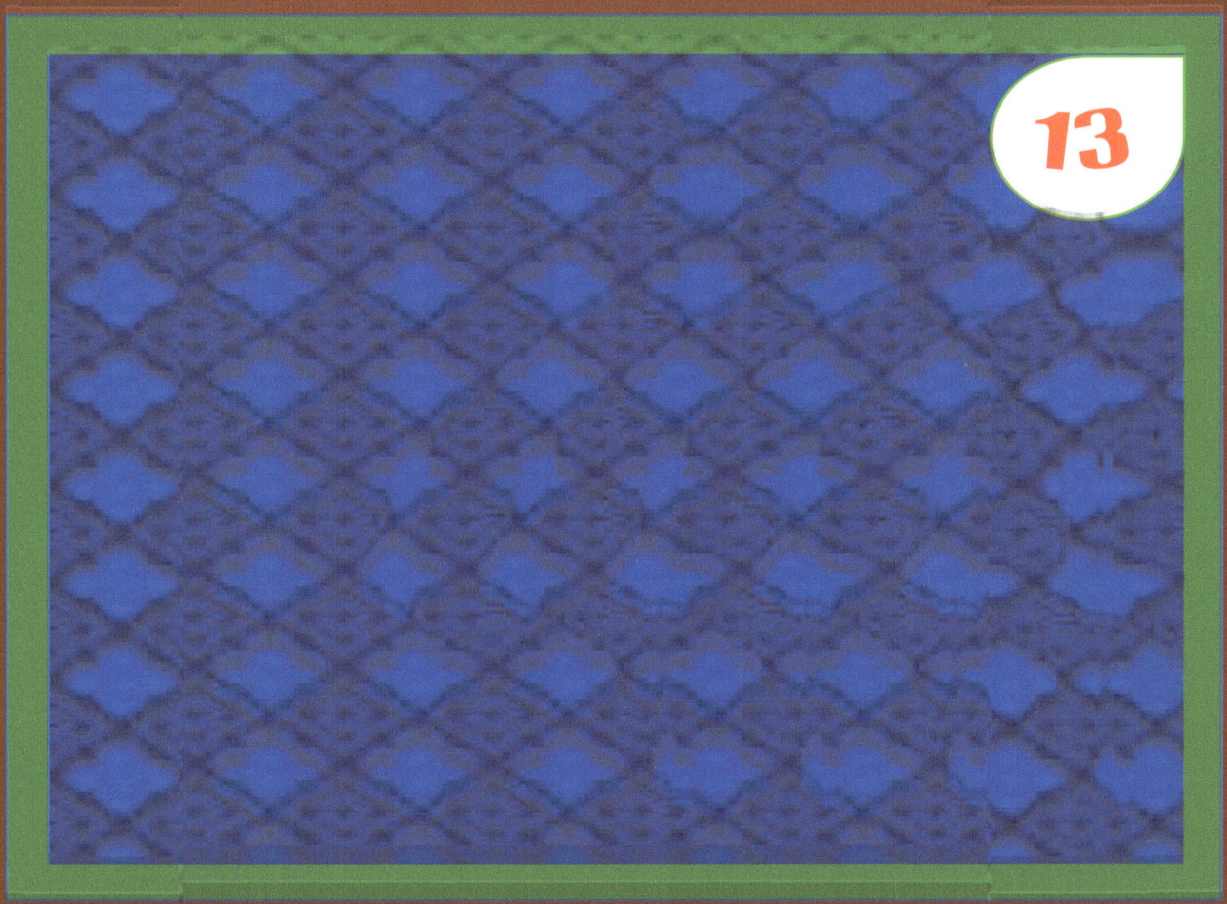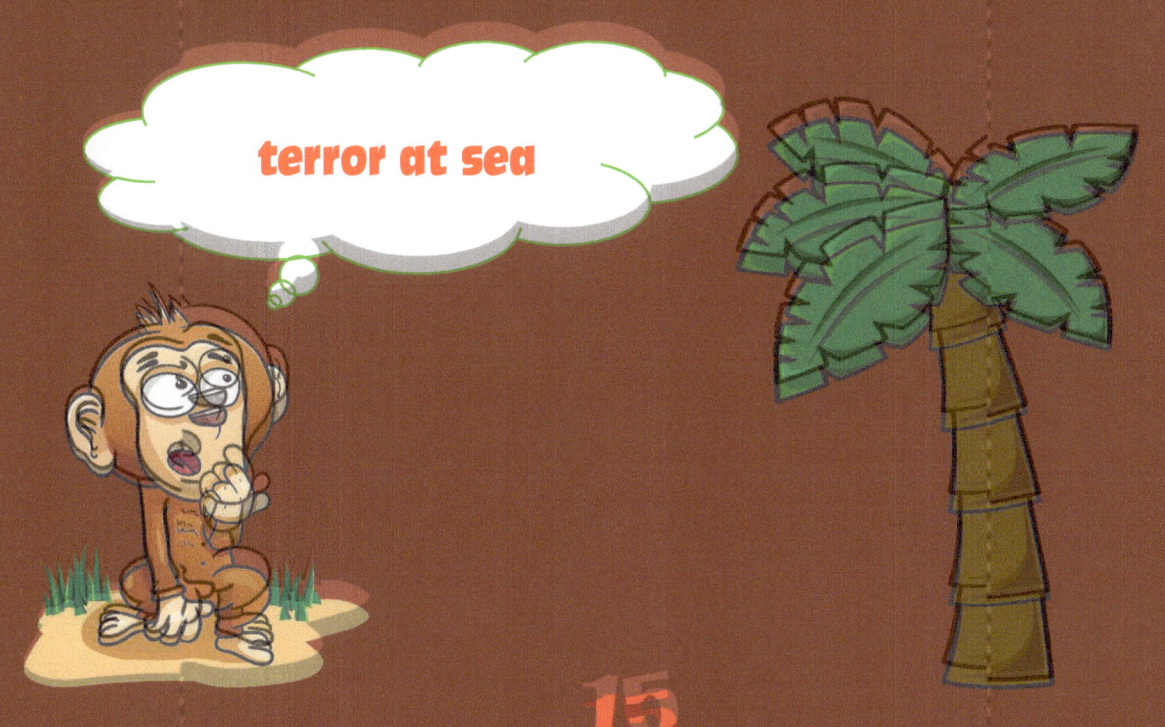

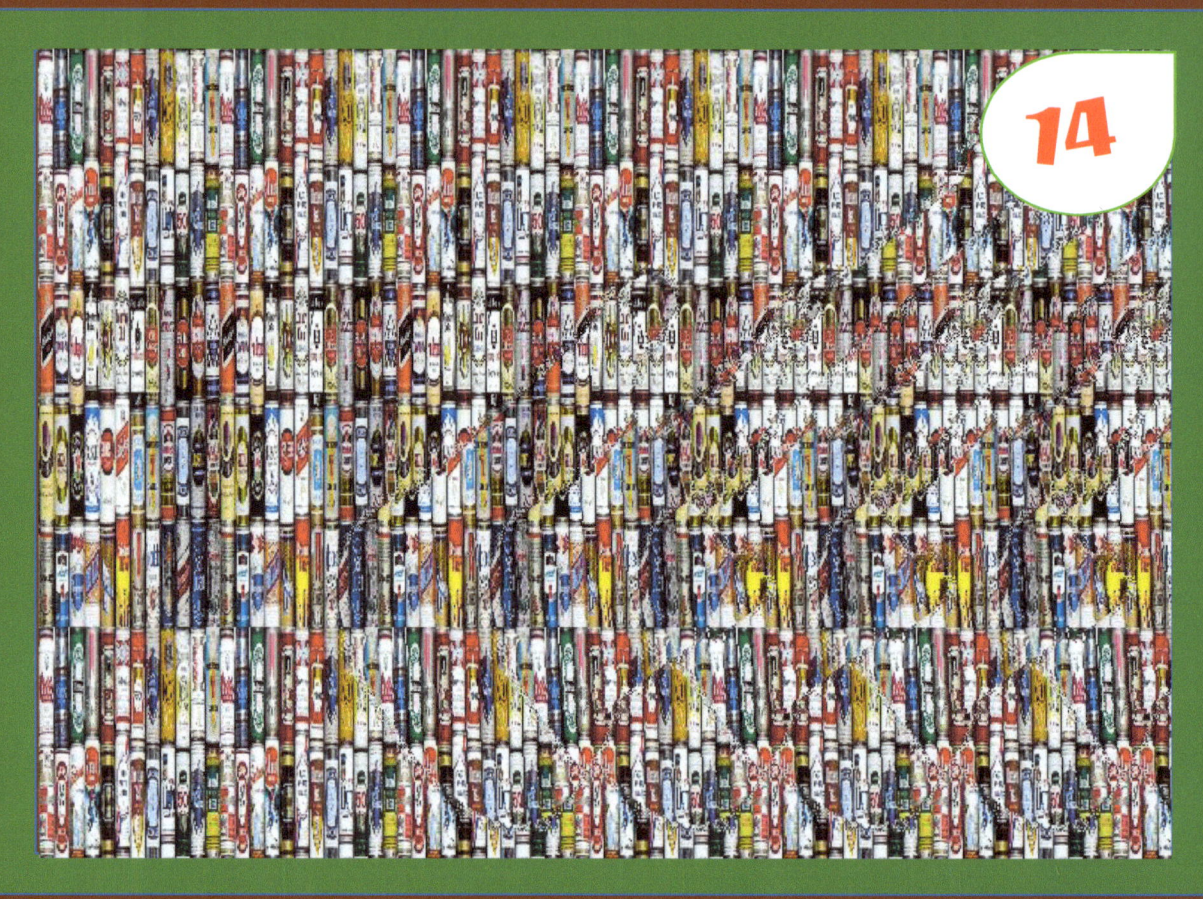

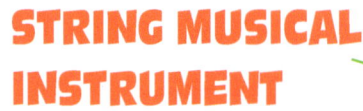

STRING MUSICAL INSTRUMENT

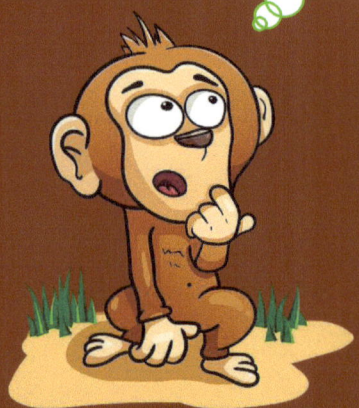

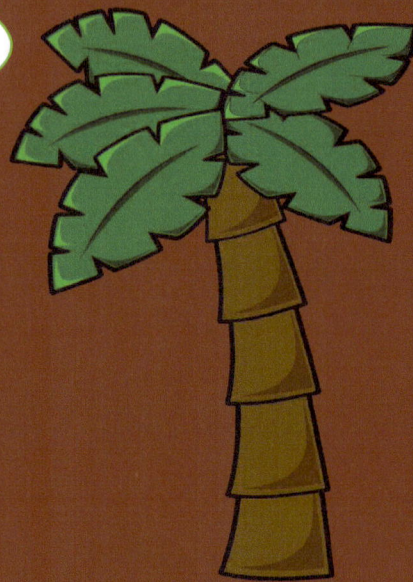

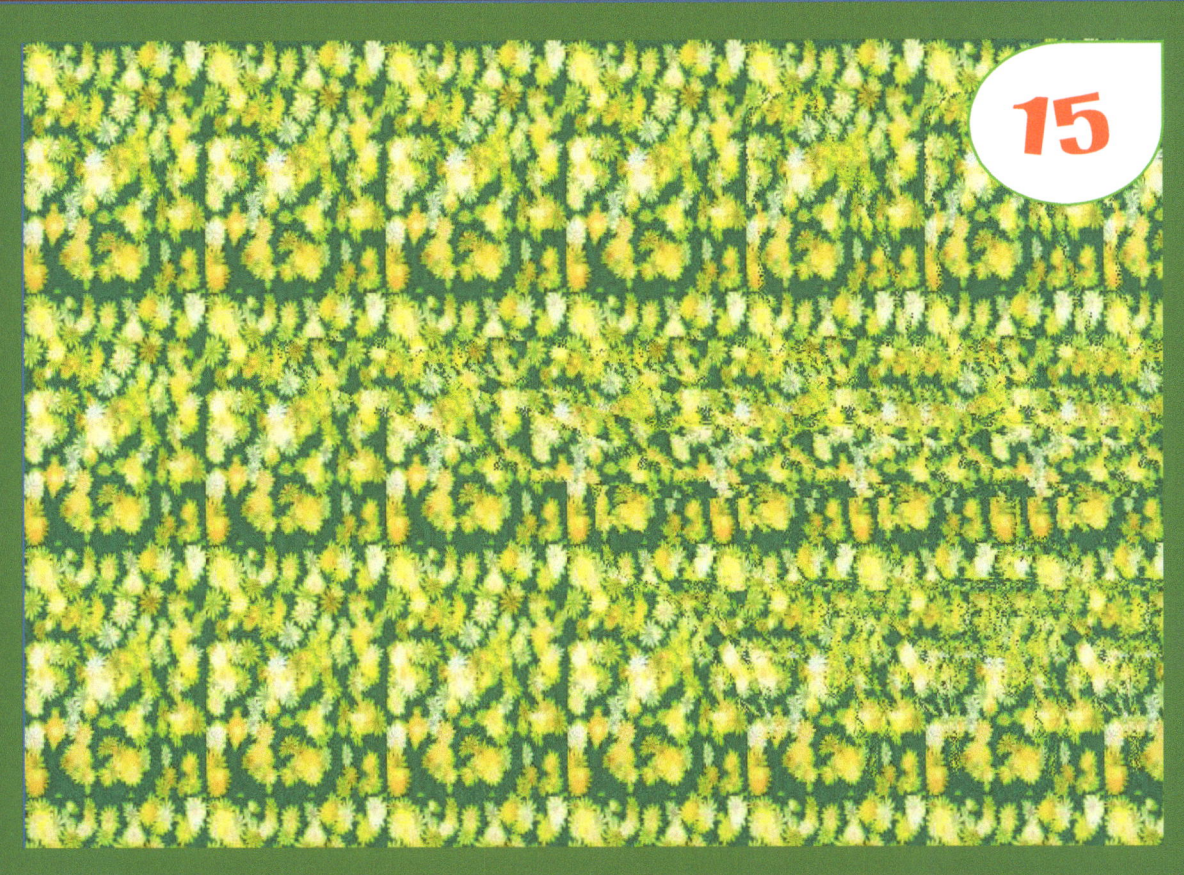
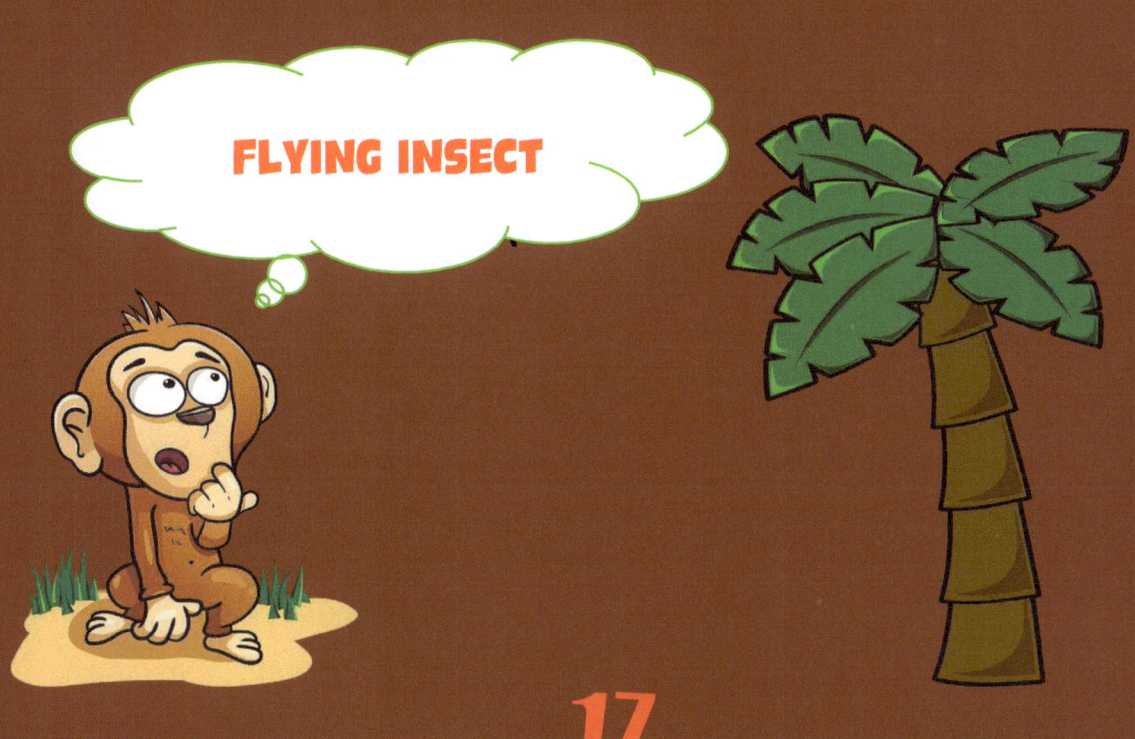

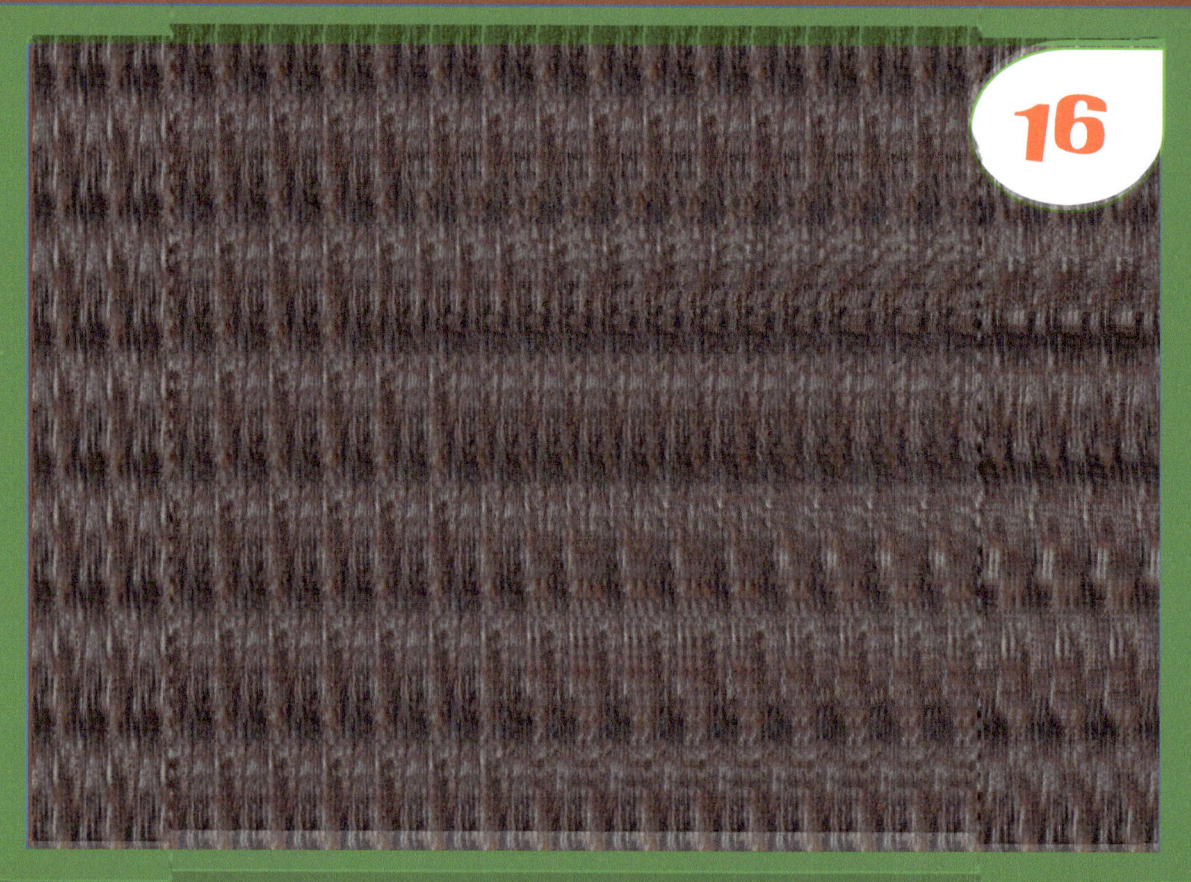

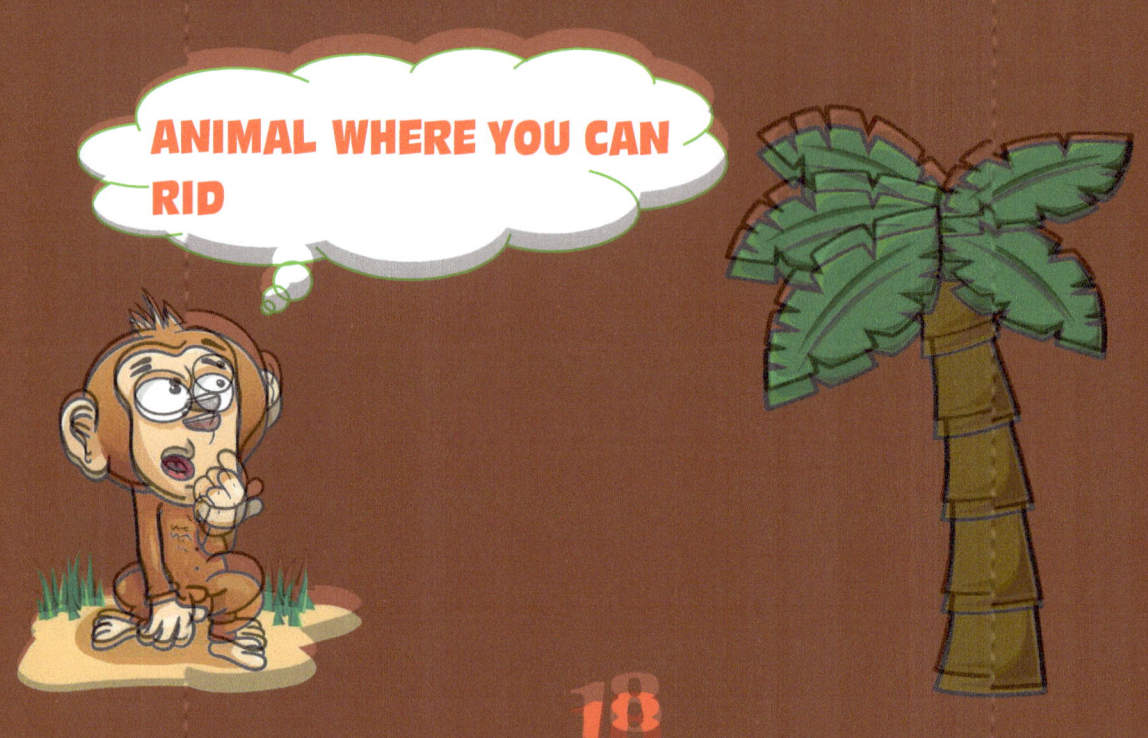

ANIMAL WHERE YOU CAN RID

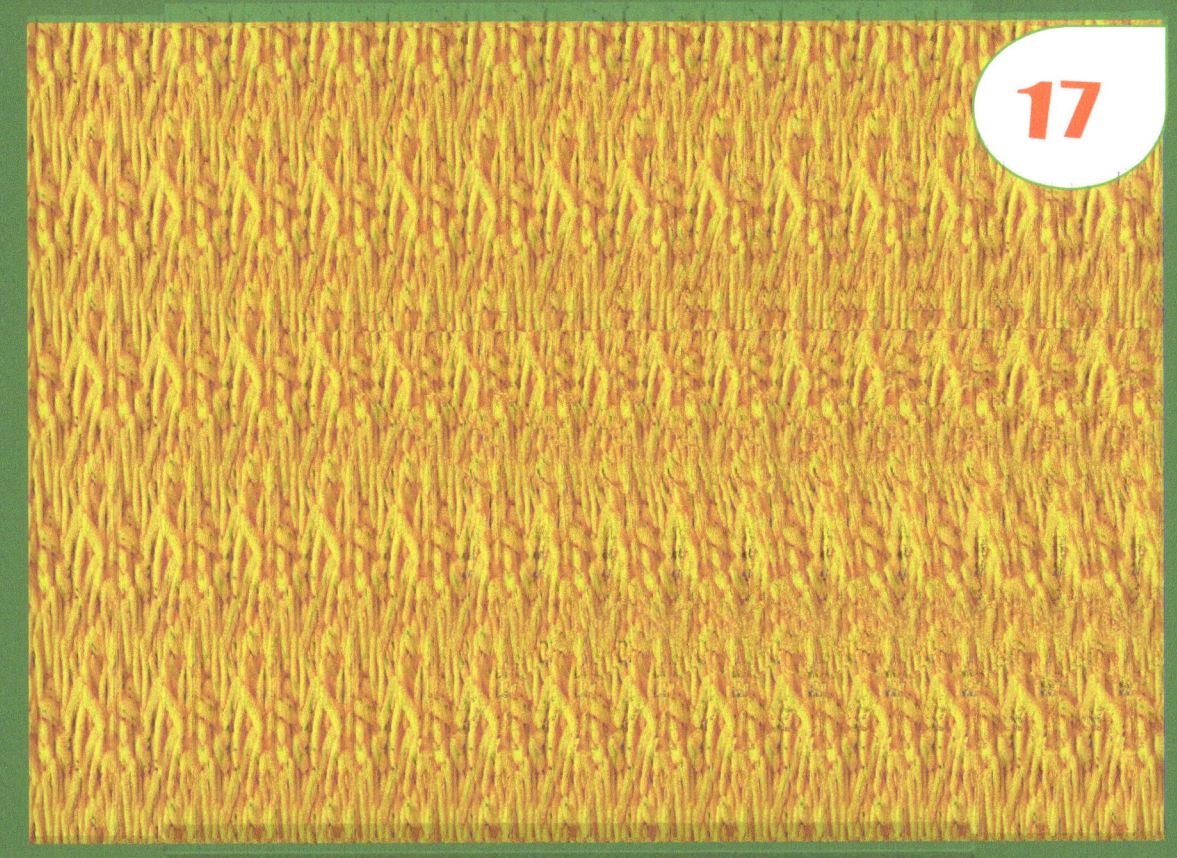
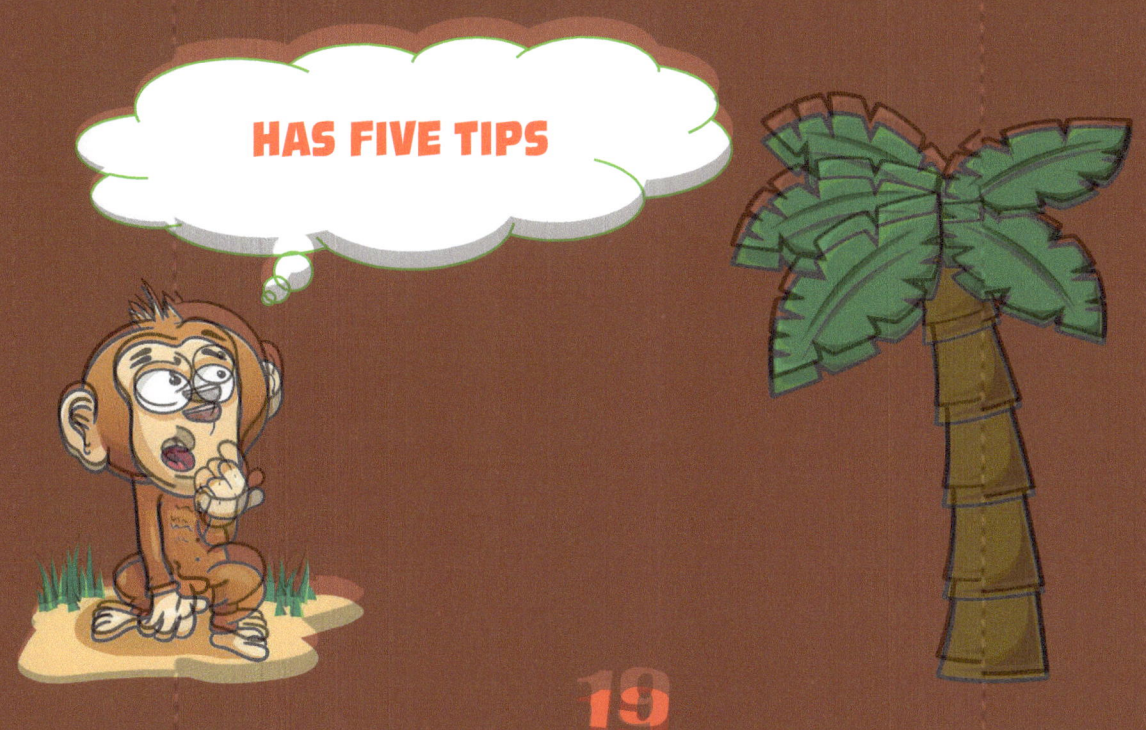

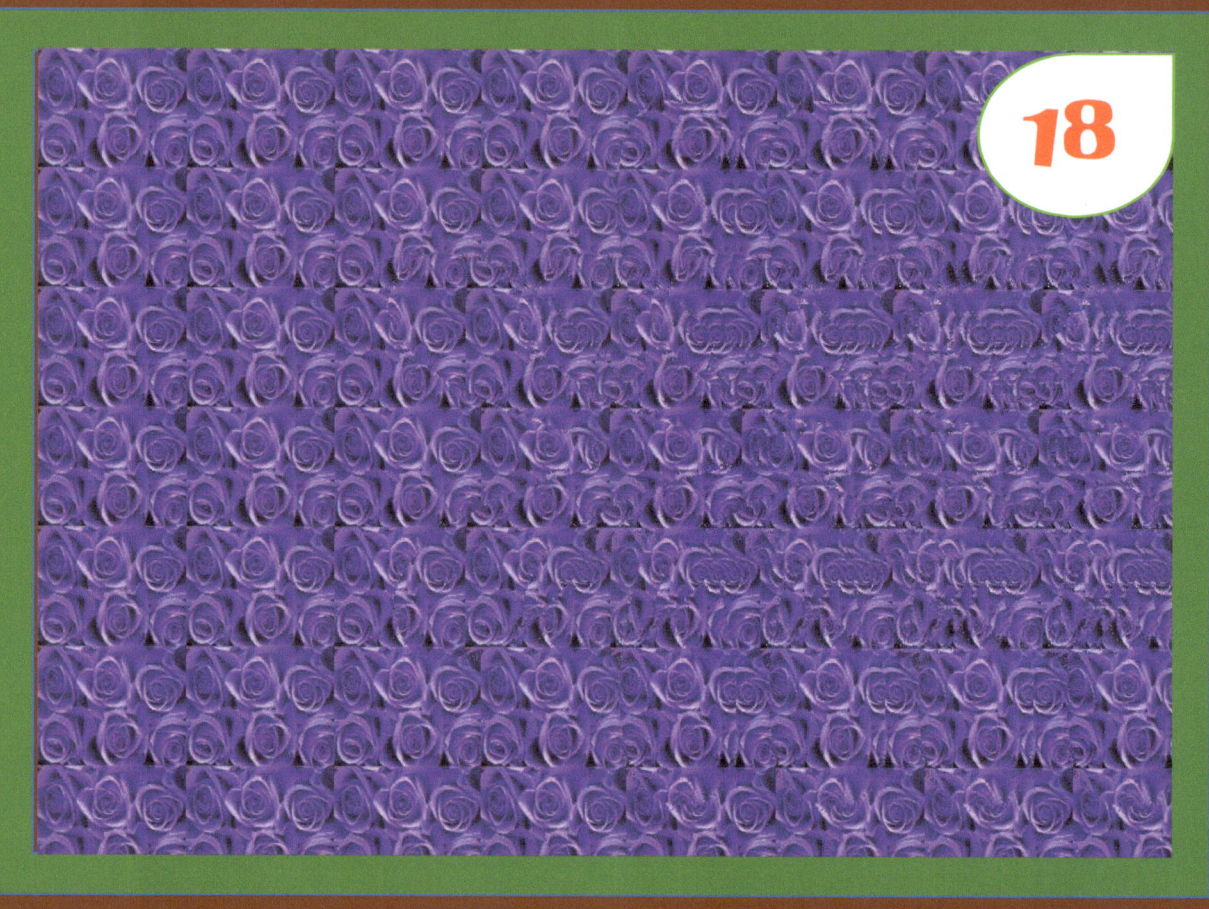

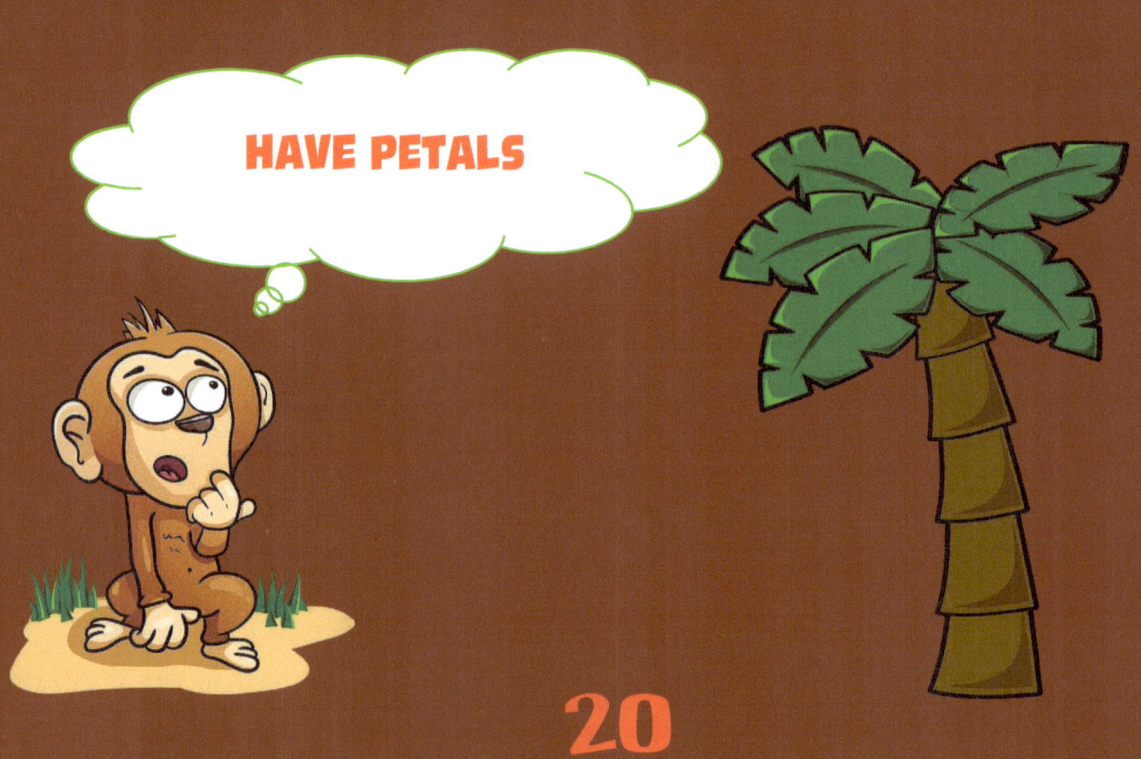

HAVE PETALS

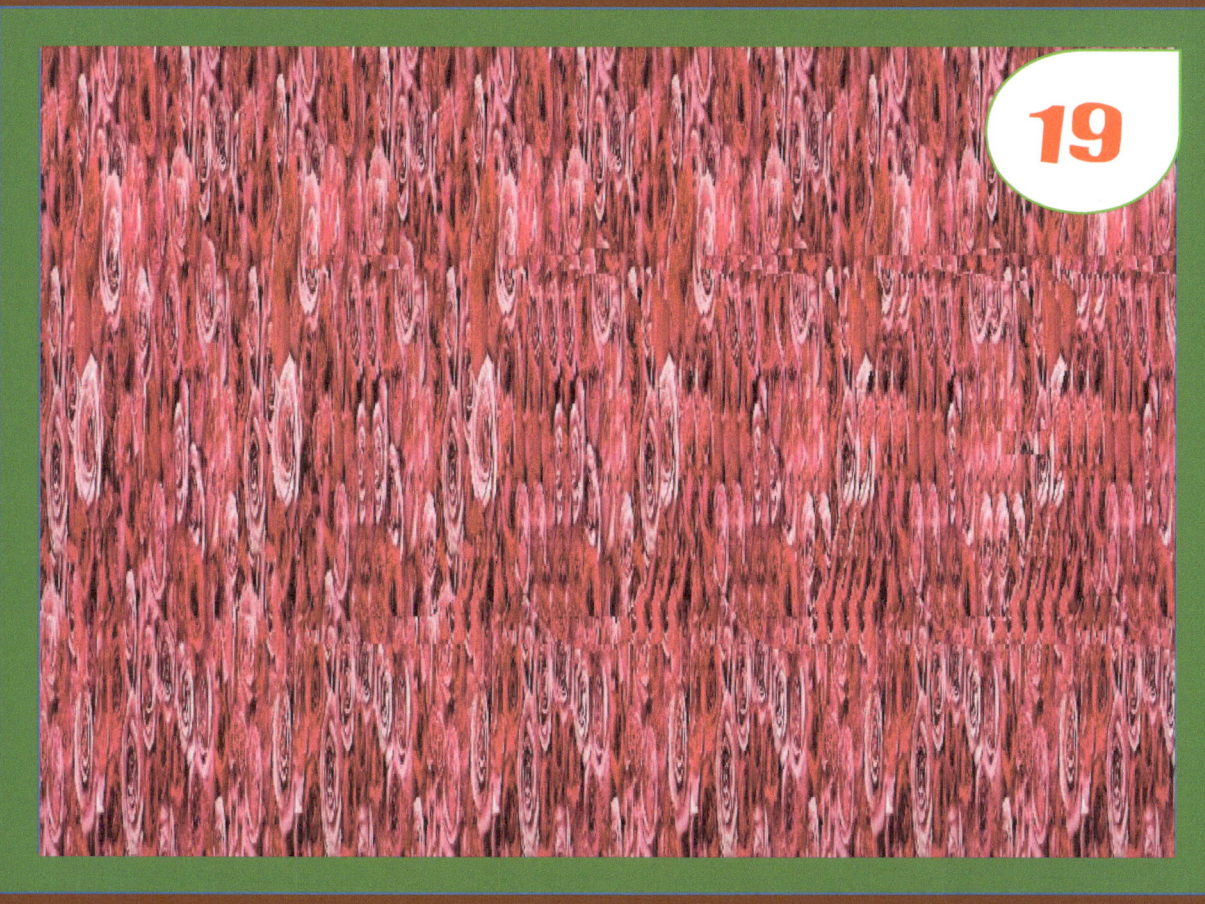

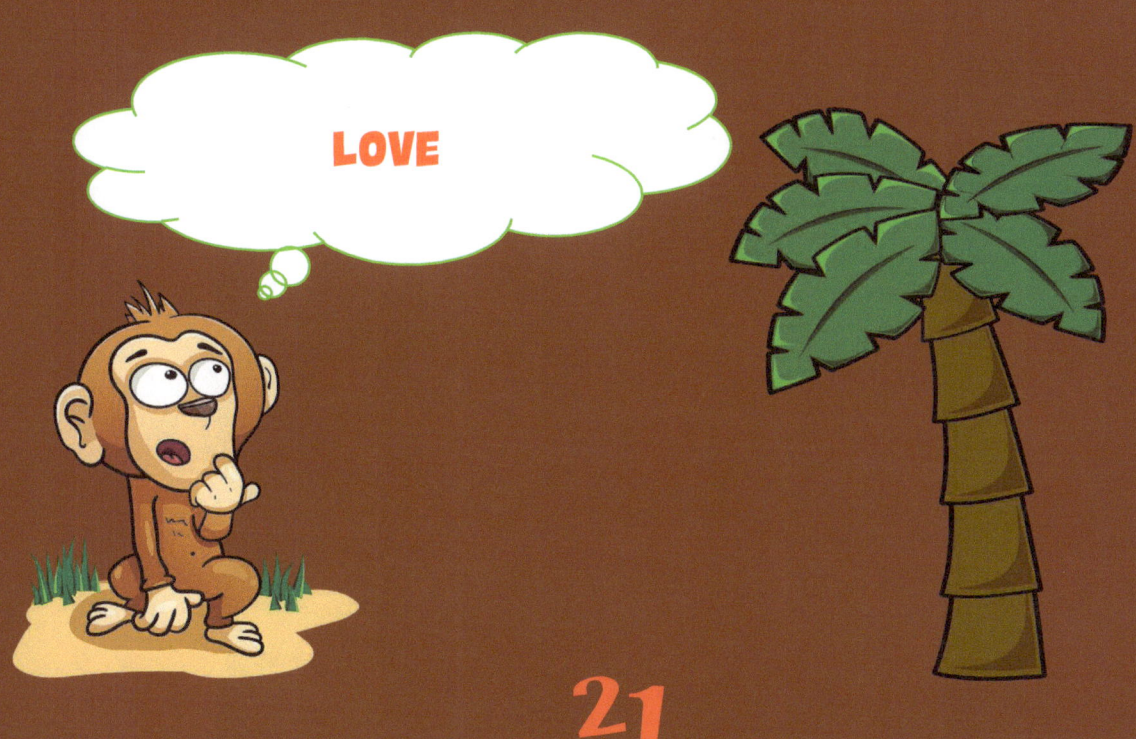

LOVE

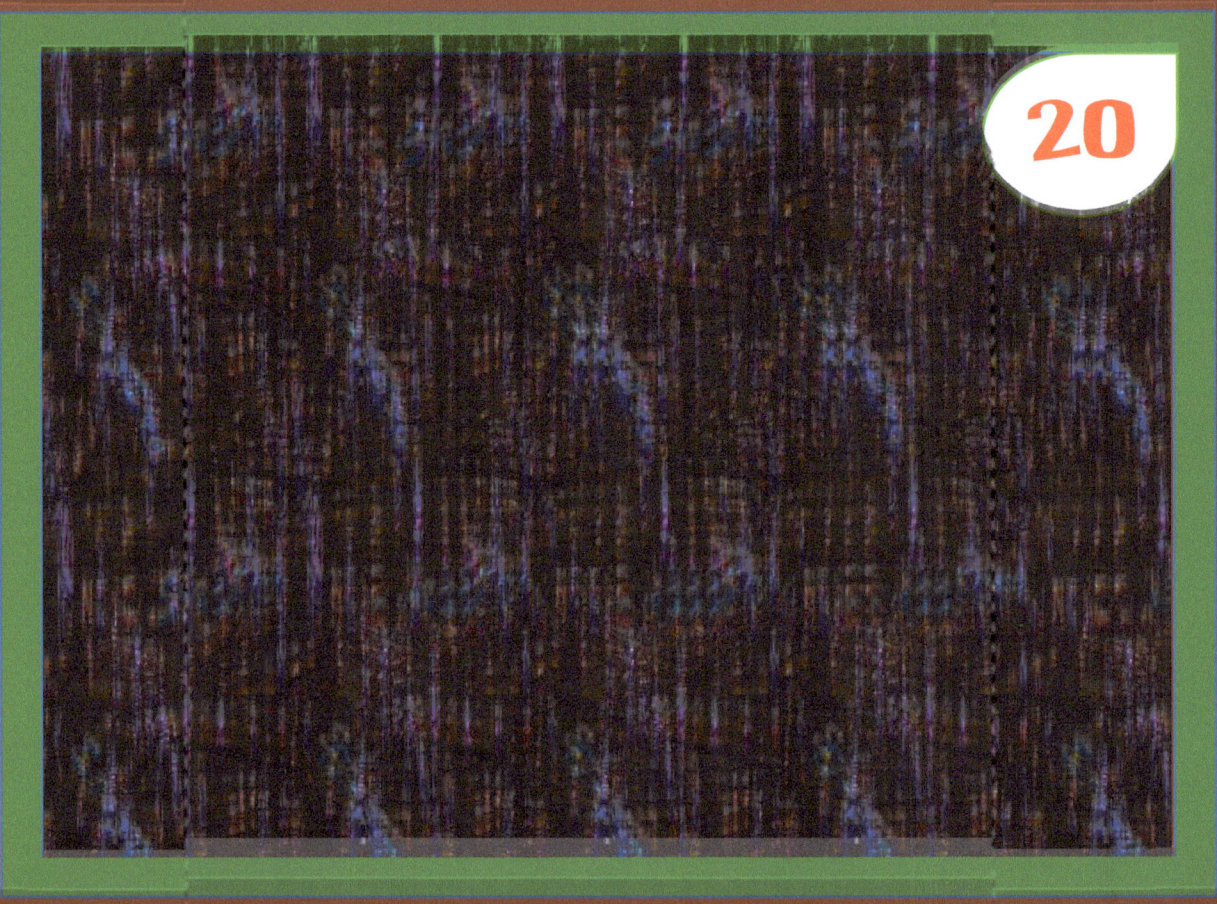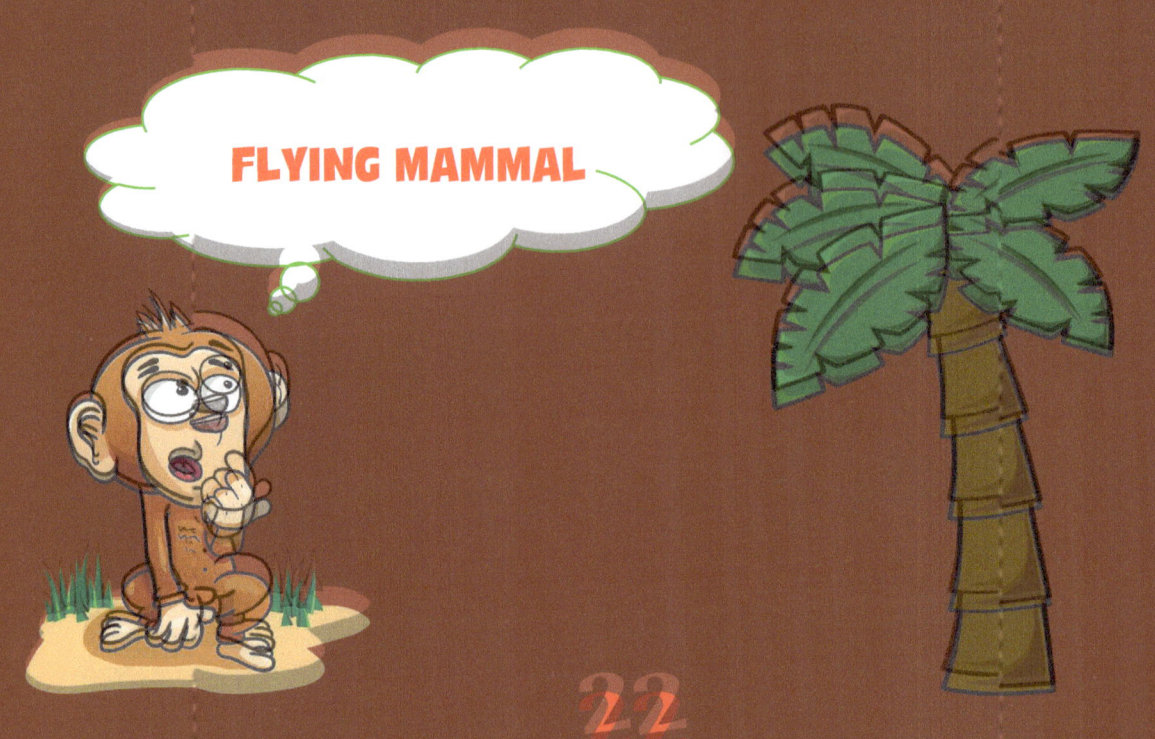

FLYING MAMMAL

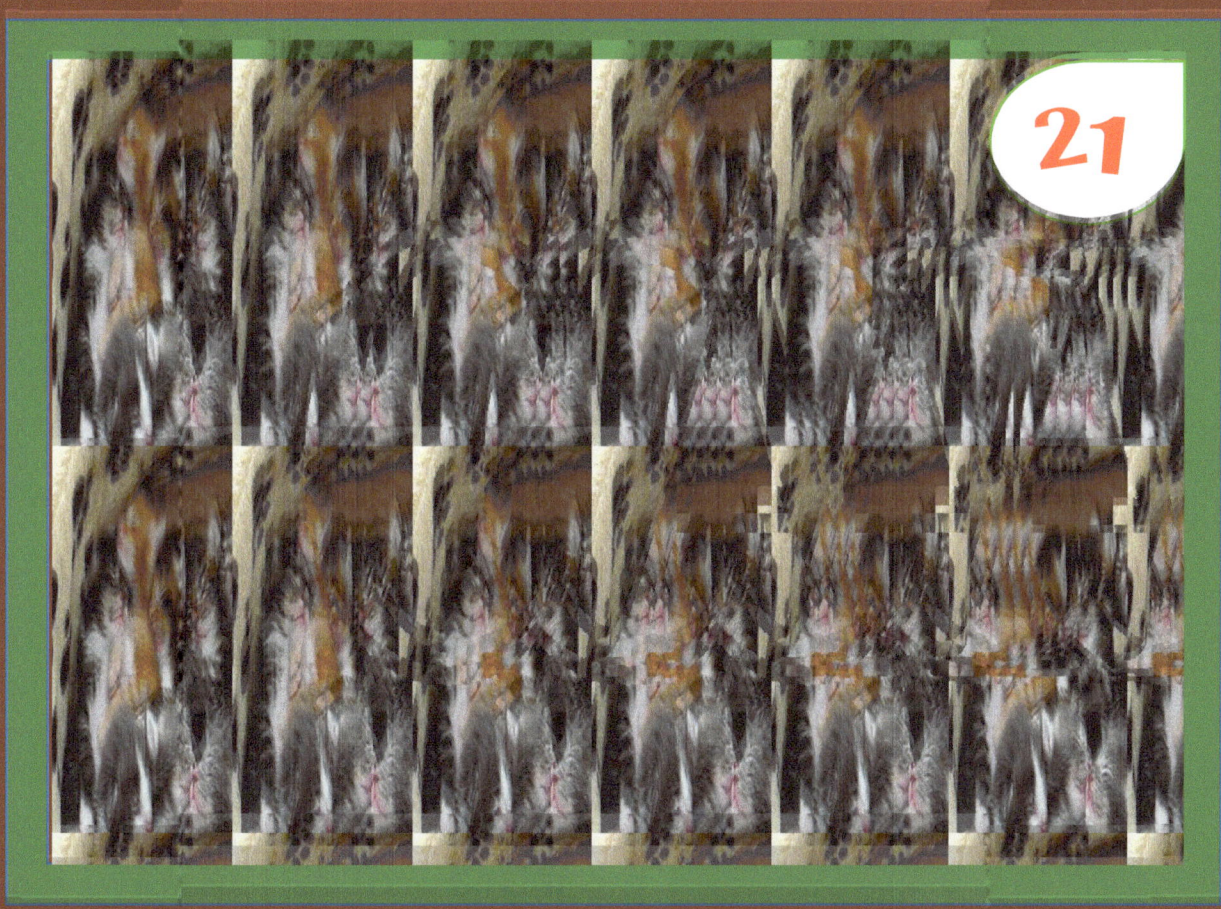

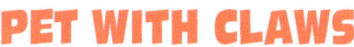

PET WITH CLAWS

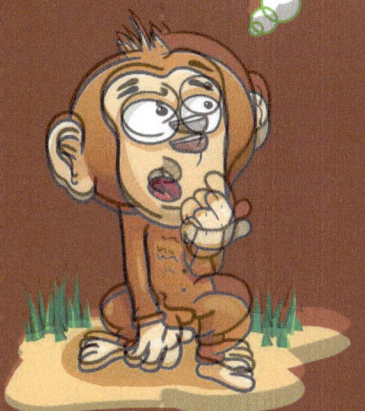
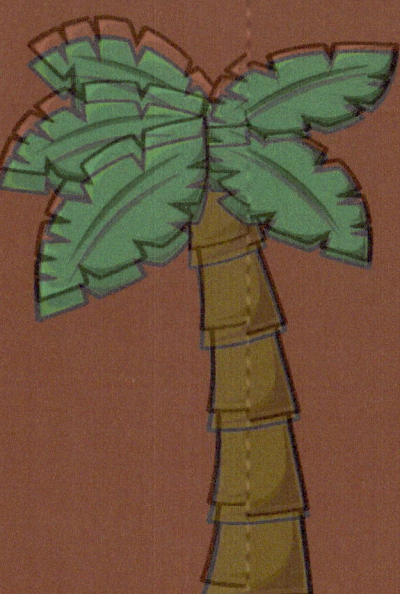

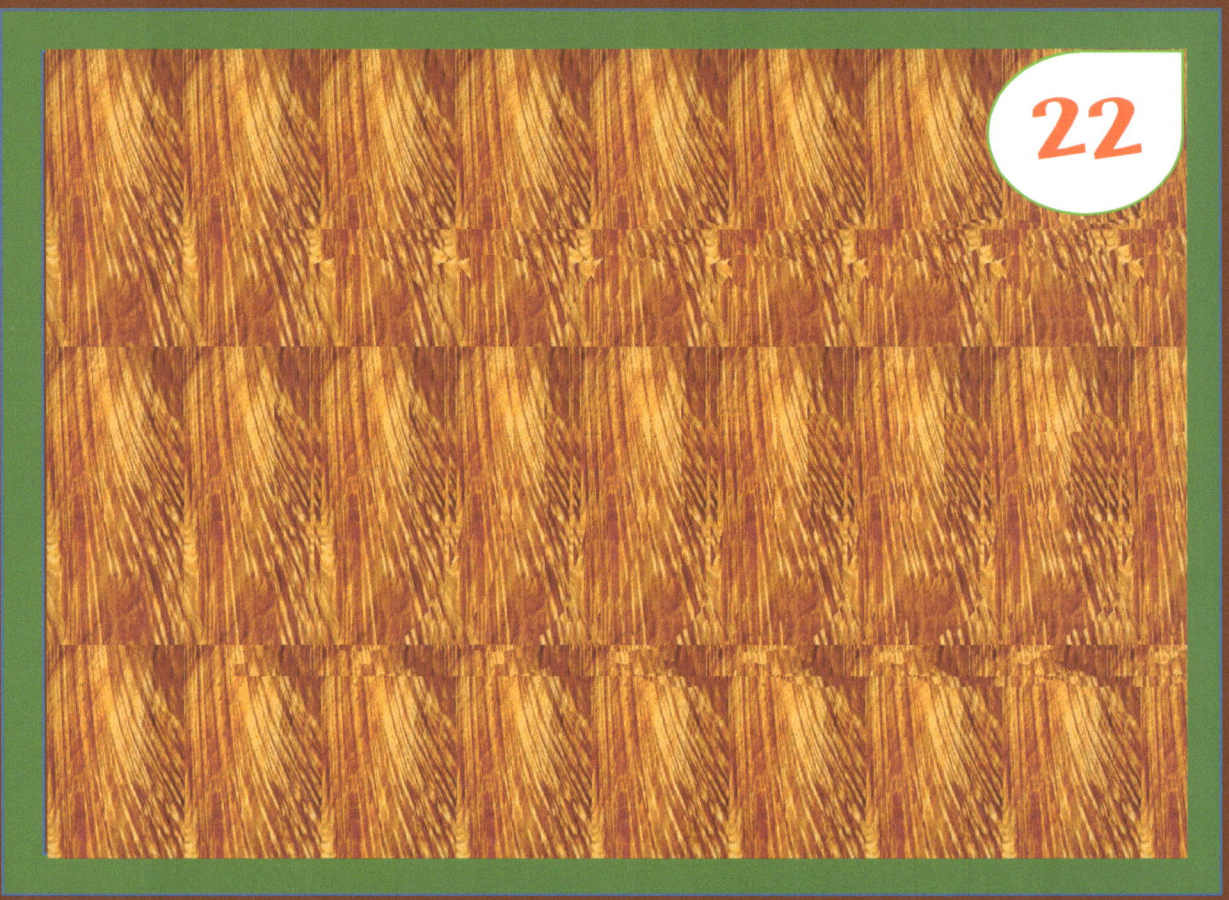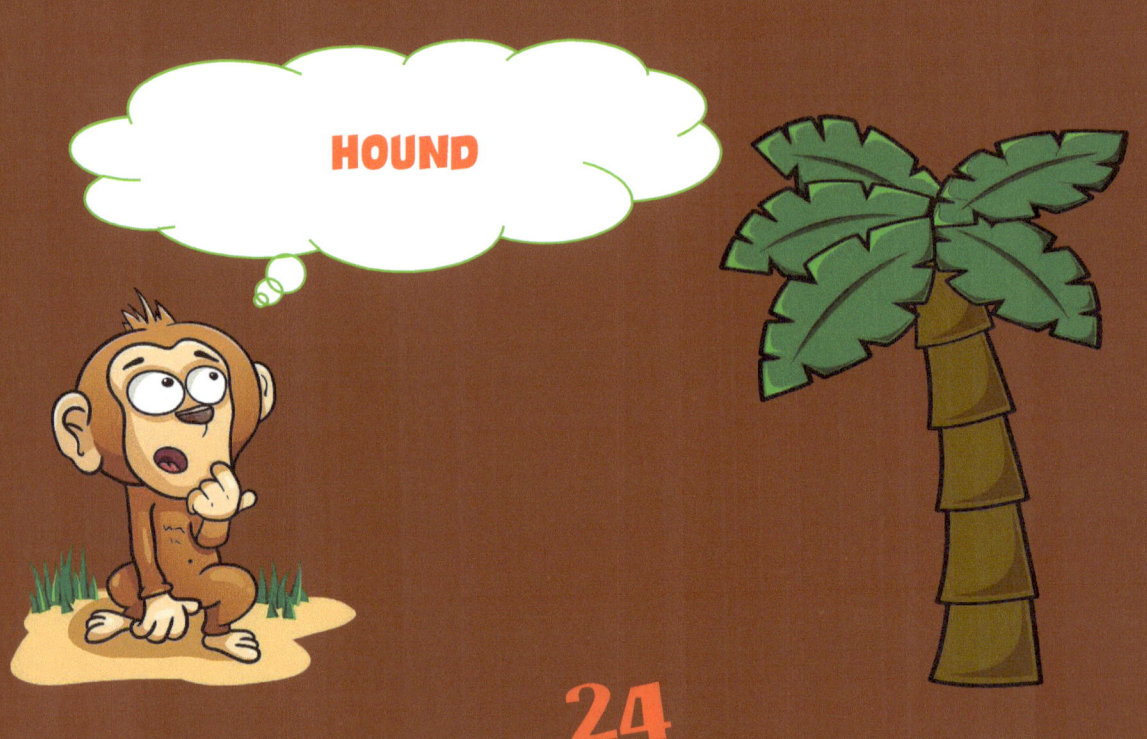

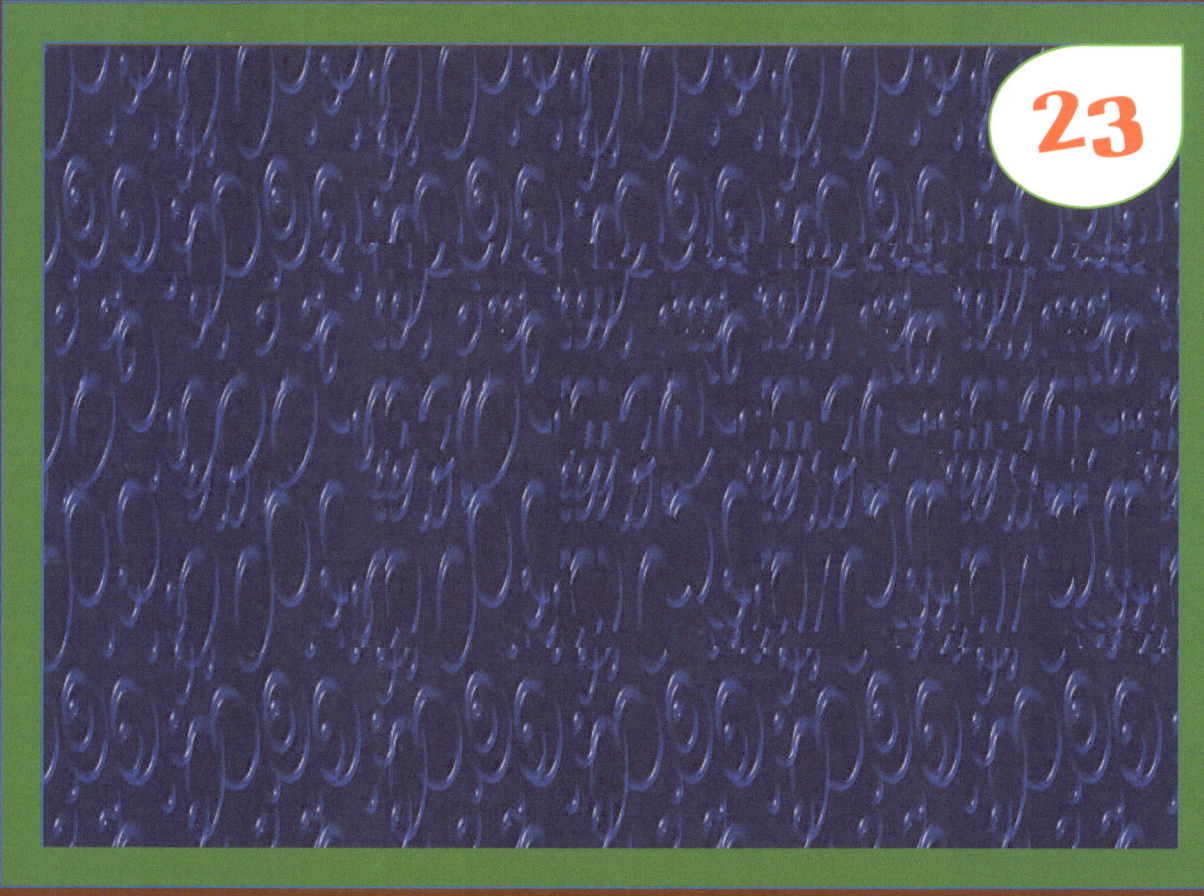

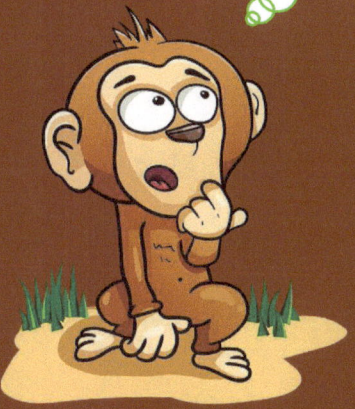

LIVES IN THE SEA

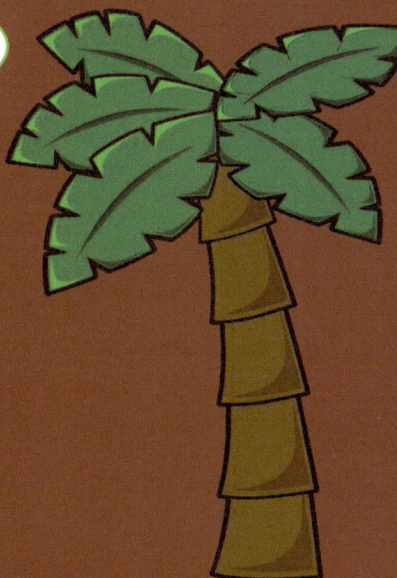

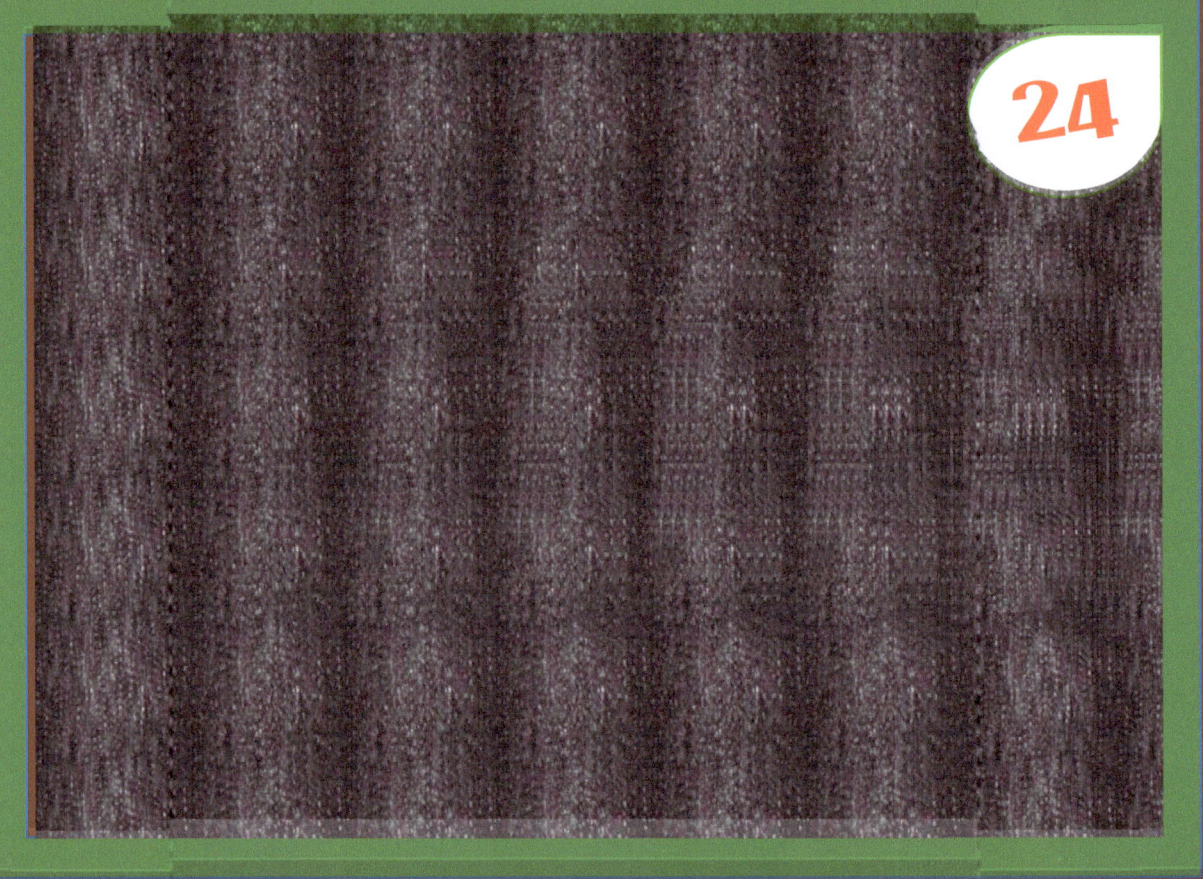
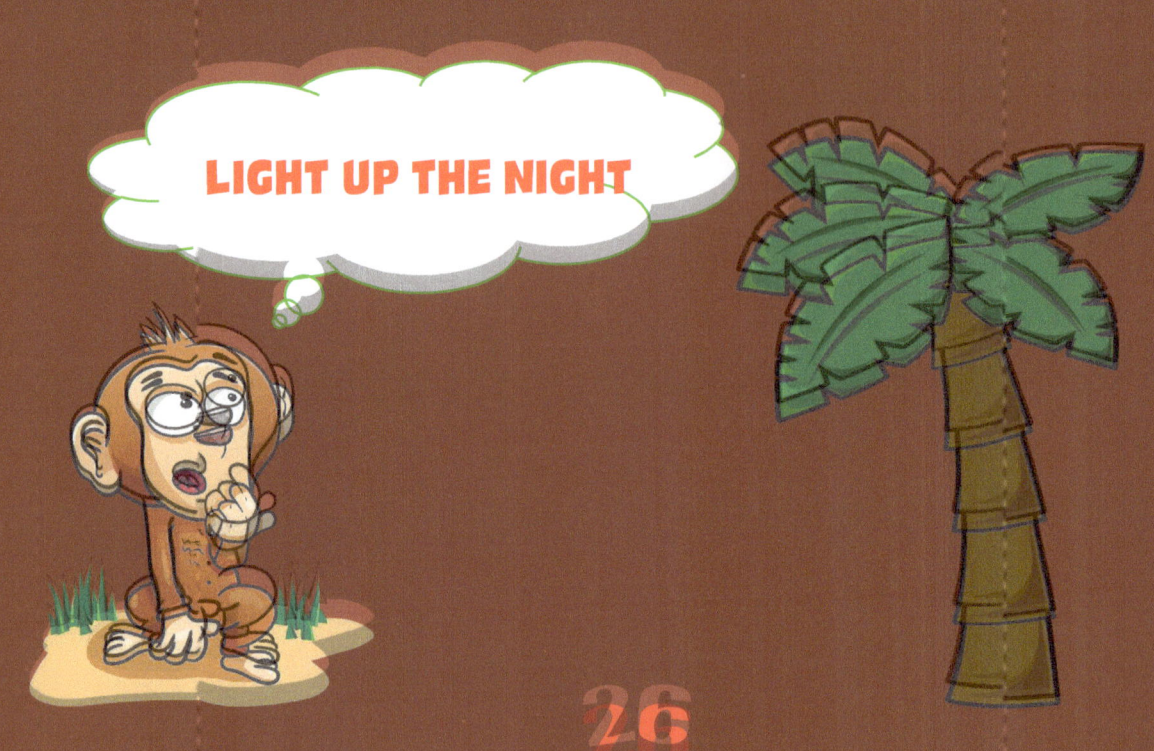

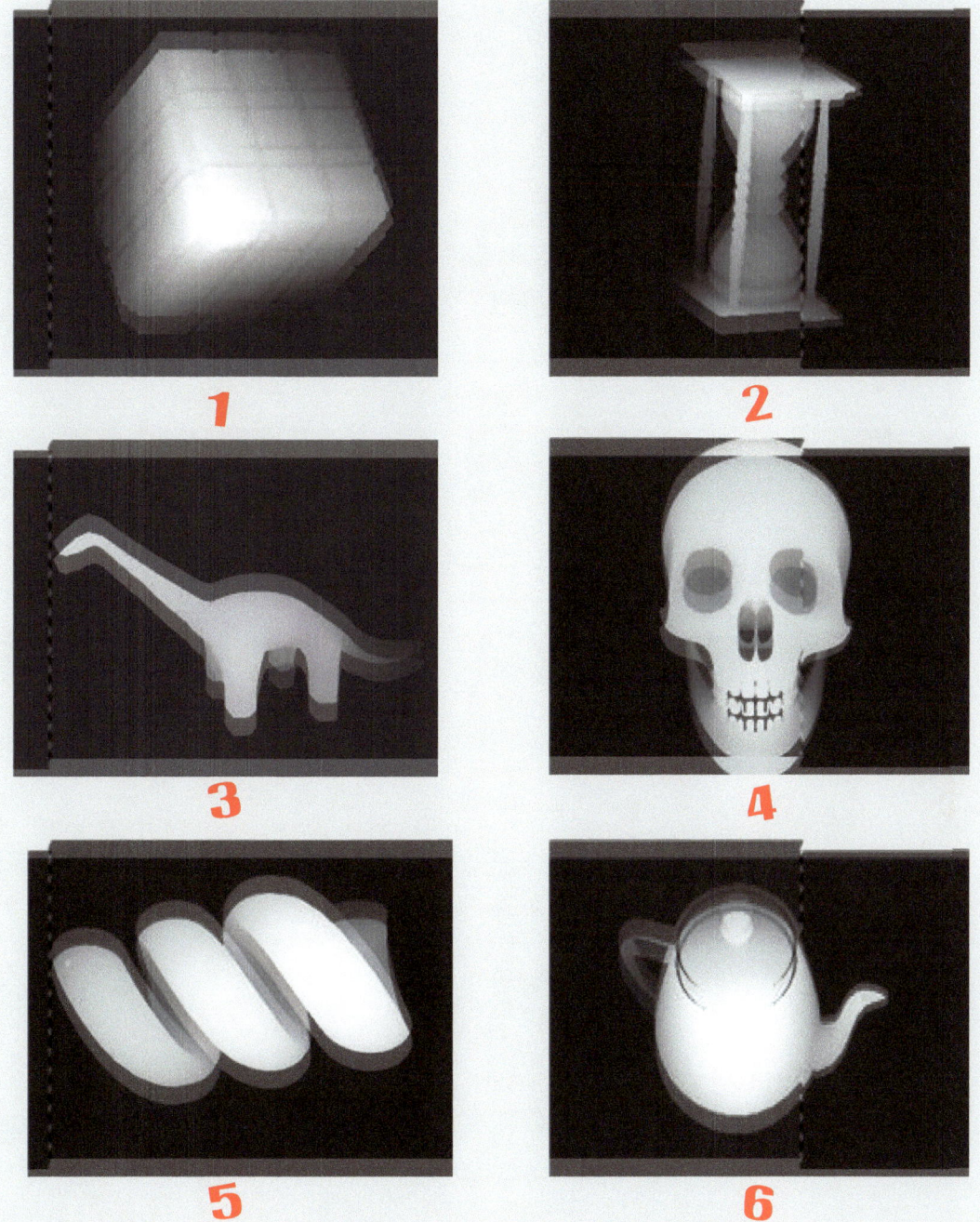

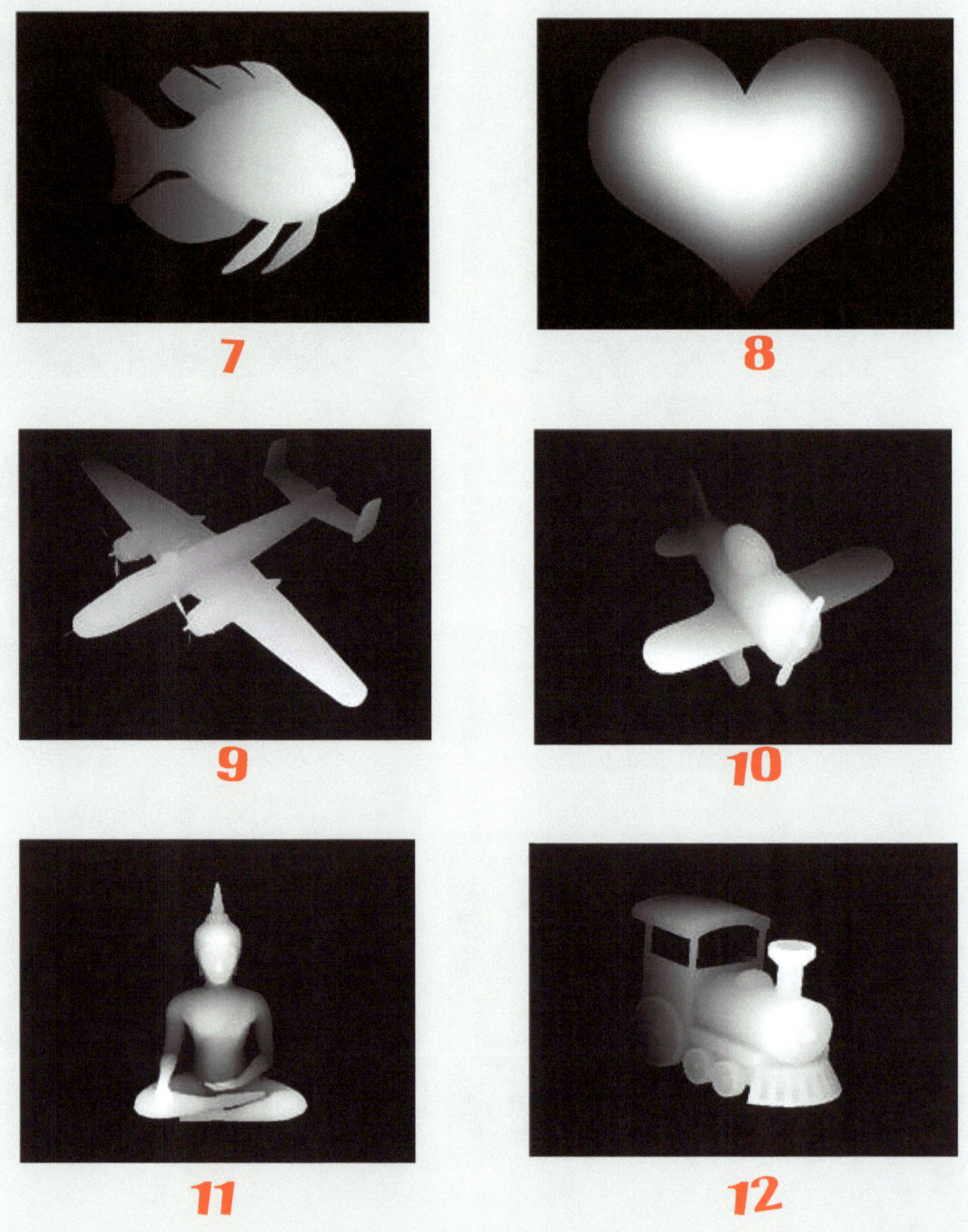

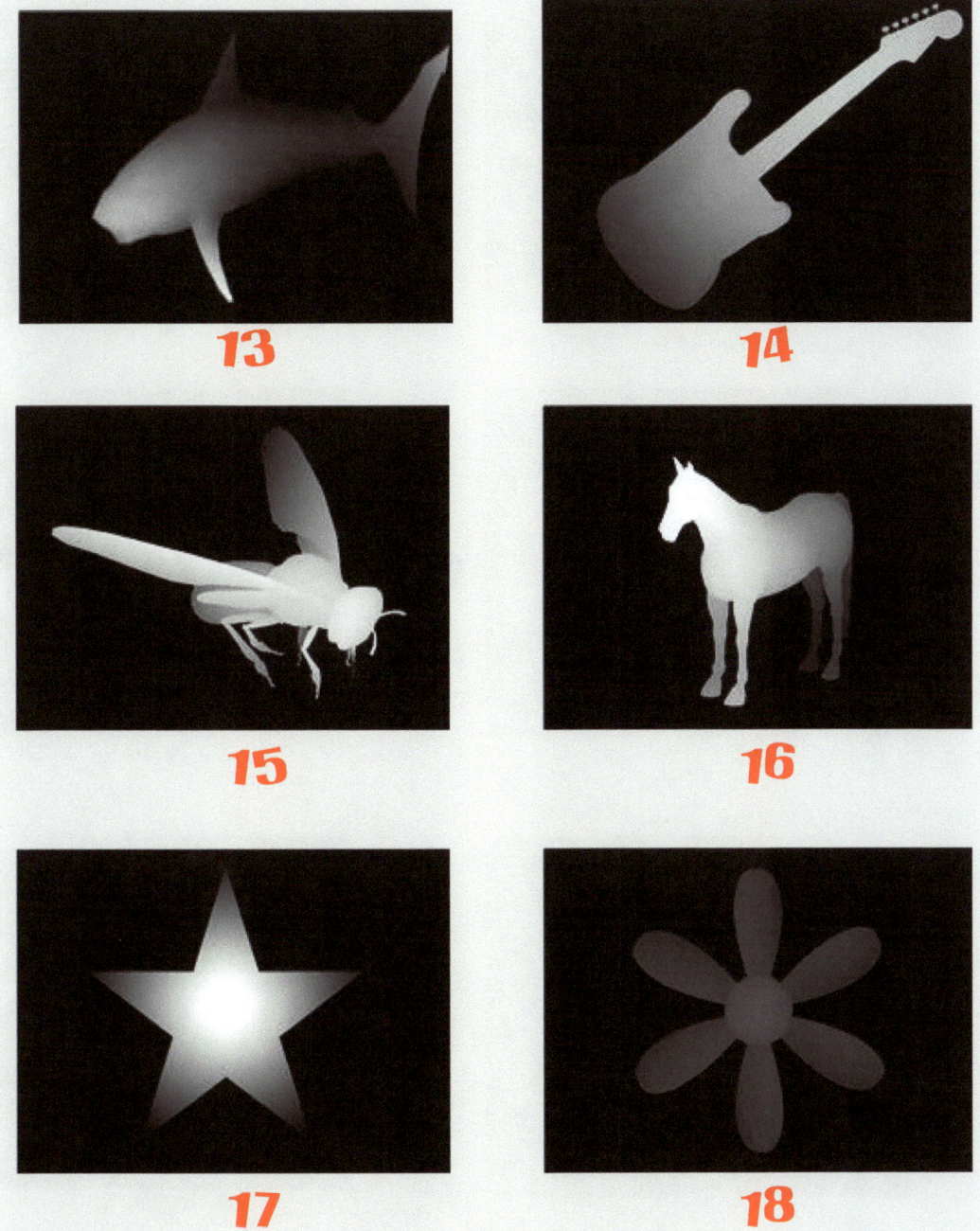

19

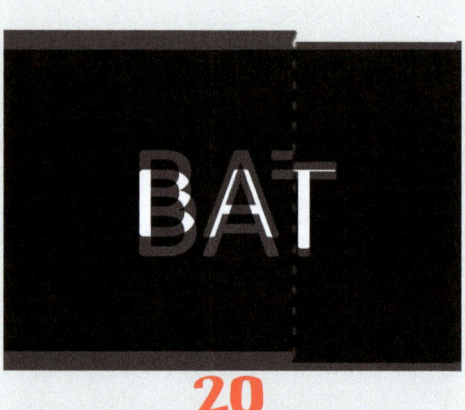
20

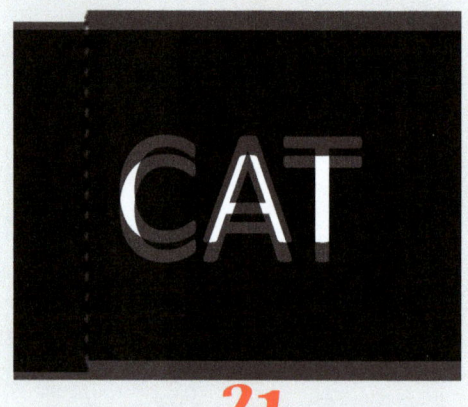
21

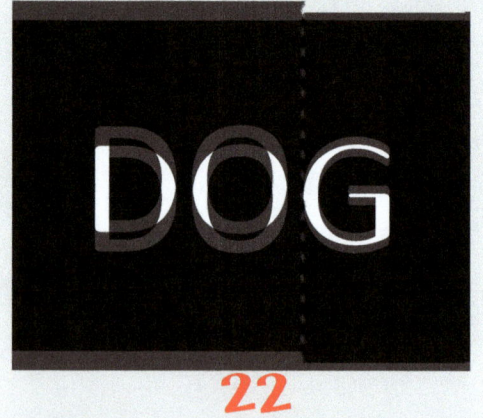
22

23

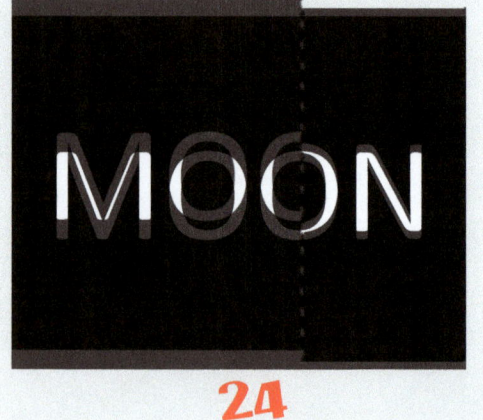
24

www.ingramcontent.com/pod-product-compliance
Lightning Source LLC
Chambersburg PA
CBHW051940210526
45473CB00006B/2323